In Spirit and In Truth

In Spirit and In Truth

The Heart's Cry for Genuine Worship

Jay Thomas Walls

authorHOUSE®

AuthorHouse™
1663 Liberty Drive
Bloomington, IN 47403
www.authorhouse.com
Phone: 1-800-839-8640

Published by AuthorHouse   09/29/2012

ISBN: 978-1-4772-7305-0 (sc)
ISBN: 978-1-4772-7306-7 (e)

Library of Congress Control Number: 2012917661

Dedication

To my dearest Erica
And all like her who long to worship the Lord
In spirit and in truth

Acknowledgements

In any project of this magnitude, several people need to receive my gratitude for their continued support in my spiritual journey and who have impacted my life in such a way that has made me into the man I have now become.

To the brother and sister in Christ who literally picked me up out of the gutter and became a picture of God's love and grace for which I will be eternally grateful for, Dave and Lisa Ubert, I will never cease to cherish your friendship.

To the obedient men and women who confirmed this project through a word and for the support you have given to my ministry, Bob and Susan Heine, Vicki Gumina and Laurel Harmon.

To the couple who for some reason has always shown their support and have inspired me to reach farther than what I believe I could go, Rev. Peter and Doris Fischer, thank you for believing in me.

To a fellow musician who has no idea as to the impact of being an example of a worshiper for me, Jason Upton, I appreciate your heart and the passion you bring to the ministry of worship.

To my church family at New Season Community Church in Belgium, Wisconsin, who accepted my tribe as family and overwhelmingly, has shown their support.

To the people who continually put up with me and share life with me in ways that others are not privileged to, David and Robin Brunnquell.

To the men I am accountable to in all of life and who share this passion for worship and simply knowing God wholeheartedly, Ron Bush and Ron Defore.

Jay Thomas Walls

Special thanks to Nancy Hise who selflessly gave time to prayerfully lend insight and the gift of editing for this project.

To John Link Studios (www.jonathonlinkstudios.com), thanks once again, John, for blessing us with your amazing gift in capturing God's beauty through photography as seen on the cover.

To the people who have been on every leg of this journey pressing me forward when I did not believe I could go any farther, Mom and Dad, I am blessed to have parents who believe in me the way that you do.

In no way could this book have become a reality without the support, love and encouragement from a loving wife and children. Words cannot express my gratitude to my wife, Erica, and our children—Nathan, Kylie, Hannah, Benjamin, Jeremiah, Josiah, and Emma, as you have put up with so much, but you never failed to show your love to me.

Finally, to the One who has given me the freedom to experience the greatest privilege in the entire universe, Jesus Christ, may my desire to know You always live up to the life I am living for You.

Table of Contents

Introduction

Let's clear the air. I have been a hypocritical, lying, manipulating, thieving, lustful, prideful, boastful, arrogant, idolatrous and selfish man. Now that we are crystal clear about the failures of my past before and after my conversion experience, you can feel at ease that I am writing from the perspective of a man who understands who he is in light of himself and in light of the grace of God. I've traveled the road of brokenness and failure which has shaped me into the person I am today. Along my journey I have been a disappointment to those who had once looked up to me and broken the hearts of those who were once closest to me. I have literally destroyed the dreams of loved ones and banished the dreams that God once birthed in my heart. Sadly, this is part of the legacy that I have left behind.

This book is a result of those broken pieces being made into the image of who I am becoming in Christ. It was necessary for the patchwork that I had fashioned of myself to be renovated and made into something completely new. The pieces are still made up of the life of who I was, but now they resemble a whole new image—the image of a man who is becoming less so that Christ can become more. To understand the heart of this book and where it is going, you first must understand the heart of the writer and where he has been. Transparency is, at times, a two-edged sword. On one edge it can build a sense of trust between people. On the other edge, I open up becoming vulnerable to your judgment. It is my willingness to be transparent, however, that allows the reader to share in my passionate pursuit of the subject in this book.

As a worship leader and songwriter, I have a burning desire to find myself in the presence of the Lord. There is a great sense of longing in my heart to see others experience the intense joy of knowing the Lord in intimacy, power and truth. Although I strive to capture the reality of the worship experience in the songs that I write, it is a greater challenge to translate the passion of the heart that lies within the worship leader and songwriter.

You might ask: "What qualifies him to write a book that attempts to call the church out of its lackadaisical approach to worshipping God?" After all, I am virtually an unknown name in the music world, academic world and church world. I do not claim to be a prophet or a preacher; nor do I claim to be an authority on the subject of worship, the Bible or the things of God. In many ways, I am your average guy who makes multiple blunders as a husband, father, and follower of Jesus Christ. So why read this book?

Could the same longing existing deep in my heart exist in yours? Do you also desire to experience more in this life than you already have? It is a cry of knowing there is so much more to this walk of faith than what we are already experiencing. Your heart, like mine, has "tasted and seen" that the Lord is good and has left you longing for more of Him. This longing comes from the frustrating realization of trying to grasp the abundant life promised to us in Christ, but somehow it eludes us every time. I write from the perspective of what the Bible presents to me as a picture of a reality I desperately desire to experience: knowing Jesus Christ as He has intended me to know Him. This book is an attempt to recapture the genuine essence of worship. It is worship that will fill the hungering soul. It is worship that will quench a heart parched for the things of God. It is worship that the Father seeks—a worship of spirit and truth.

This book is a prophetic challenge. It is a call to return to the God in whom we have neglected while attempting to appease Him with a half-hearted worship, void of the presence of His Spirit and defined by our own standard of *truth*. It is a cry for a genuine, authentic, unbridled response of worship to the Giver of Life and the Lover of Our Souls. The prophet Isaiah cried out to his generation which had forsaken the practice of acceptable worship before the Lord. He revealed to them, despite their wanderings, that Yahweh was still willing to be their God if they would only return to Him as being the center of their lives. Isaiah called out to the people: *"Seek the Lord while he may be found; call on him while he is near"* (Isaiah 55:6). His still voice echoes in our day as well. In a world held captive by the spirit of Babylon, God is calling His people from the land of exile—reeking of a lukewarm, complacent and spiritually apathetic religion—to once again forcefully lay hold of the kingdom conferred upon those with "eyes to see and ears to hear." In so many ways, the church has wandered from the truth. The Bride of Christ is no longer captivated by the Spirit of the Groom; yet He faithfully calls out to His people: *"Come, all you who are thirsty, come to the waters . . . Give ear and come to me; hear me that your soul may live"* (Isaiah 55:1,3). If we are ever to become the people in whom God has intended us to be and to live the promised life that comes only through salvation and redemption, then we must heed to the Word of the Lord beckoning us to once again worship Him in spirit and in truth.

> *The Lord is the Spirit, and where the Spirit of the Lord is, there is freedom.*
> 2 Corinthians 3:17

> *If you hold to my teaching, you are really my disciples. Then you will know the truth and the truth will set you free . . . So if the Son sets you free, you will be free indeed.*
> John 8:32 and 36

Chapter One

Moving Beyond
Vanilla Worship

*Therefore come out from among their midst and
be separate says the Lord and do not touch what is
unclean and I will welcome you.*
2 Corinthians 6:17

Over the last century the American culture has redefined what worship once was. For many, worship surrounds the subject of what transpires during a church's song service. Although we may call the service in its totality a *worship* service, we carefully compartmentalize the various aspects of church life to encompass their own individual meanings. The typical church service includes our praise and worship, sermon, offering, occasional attention to the ordinances of the church, and if time allows, prayer, offertory or special music, and a concluding blessing. Enter the doors of any evangelical church and you will find similar formats, songs, music styles, preaching emphasis and a push to become a more relevant community to the world around them. It is a conglomeration of the Willow Creek, Saddleback, John Maxwell and George Barna church growth strategies that shapes the face of contemporary worship. For a God who offers more than the *Thirty-One Flavors* of the typical church setting, the Body of Christ remains content to indulge ourselves in America's favorite flavor of worship: *Evangelical Vanilla.*

What does this metaphoric example have to do with the subject of worship? Think about it. Doesn't the idea of simply taking a vanilla approach to worship seem like an inviting, open, inclusive and prodigious idea? In the world of ice cream, vanilla goes with everything. In the church world, it allows us to take the pure flavor of worship and add things to it in order to change the taste, presentation and overall appeal of the experience.

This is best illustrated in one of my past experiences as a worship leader in a local congregation. Whenever a church experiences a change in leadership it will inevitably bring new challenges to the church body. If a church has been doing something the same way for years and suddenly the security of commonplace is threatened, people will become critical of whatever changes may come to pass, even if it is a necessary change to move the church forward. With that said, this was not one of those cases. Historically, this church had a reputation of experiencing a free flowing, intimate, passionate response to worship. The problem, however, in this type of atmosphere was that the modern day seeker had a difficult time finding this church as a comfortable place to spend an hour on Sunday morning. The new leadership pursued making the church a place where visitors could relate to the worship service which created conflict among the pastor and worshippers.

Some of you may ask, "Isn't that a good thing?"

My answer may surprise you. Absolutely not! If an unbeliever can relate to your worship service then I question if true worship is taking place. 1 Corinthians 2:14 states, *"The man without the Spirit does not accept the things that come from the Spirit of God, for they are foolishness to him and he cannot understand them, because they are spiritually discerned."* We cannot try to make something acceptable to those who do not "accept the things" of God; unless of course, if what we are doing is void of the Spirit.

Worship was not created to cater to man but to glorify God. A focus upon the things that makes *man* feel good and considers what man wants, thinks, or feels, places man at the center of worship. In essence, this is idolatry. Worship must solely be centered upon the Lord if it is to be considered *genuine worship*.

For some reason the church has shied away from allowing the unbridled expression of worship to take place in the midst of their services in fear of offending those in attendance. Scripture states in John 4:24 that God is the only One who determines how He is to be worshipped. We have taken the purity of vanilla and decided to mix in our own flavors in an attempt to make the worship experience more palatable. This is the beauty of evangelical vanilla. It can be best described as a special formulation of complex flavors blended into a rich, traditional vanilla-like mixture resulting in the perfect concoction that appeals to any appetite. The modern day church appears to be bent on creating a relational or relevant church experience for unbelievers and the lines between *worship* and *evangelism* have become blurred.

Worship isn't something that can be relevant or relational to the world. This thought has caused me to consider a seldom asked question: "Is the Body of Christ doing unbelievers a great disservice by allowing them to feel as if they are participating in the worship of a holy God when their hearts are far from Him?" Contrary to today's approach to worship, the biblical model of the first century church did not promote seeker sensitive services. Instead, the church went into the world and sought after the lost. Today, we reverse the pattern and present the church as an attractive place where unbelievers seek us to find out about Christ.

One of the more interesting portions of scripture that warns against the idea of making non-believers or nominal believers feel at home in the worshiping community is found in Hebrews 10:26-31:

> If we deliberately keep on sinning after we have received the knowledge of the truth, no sacrifice for sins is left, but only a fearful expectation of judgment and raging fire that will consume the enemies of God. Anyone who rejected the Law of Moses died without mercy on the testimony of two or three

3

> *witnesses. How much more severely do you think a man deserves to be punished who has trampled the Son of God underfoot, who has treated as an unholy thing the blood of the covenant that sanctified him, and who has insulted the Spirit of grace? For we know Him who said, 'It is mine to avenge;' I will repay, and again, 'the Lord will judge his people.' It is a dreadful thing to fall into the hands of the living God.*

Although this passage is at times debated over whether or not a person's salvation can be lost, a more pressing issue is too often overlooked. The writer of Hebrews warns those who would casually associate with Christianity without committing to a life-changing faith in Christ. In making unbelievers feel as if they are a part of the Body of Christ when they are not is a great injustice. The sense of comfort and security they feel in approaching God without the righteousness that comes from Christ degrades the holiness of worship. This is not to say that we should forgo the idea of being welcoming and loving to unbelievers; but in matters of worship, the church should not consider the seeker's perspective on the worship experience—it's not for them! Evangelism is for the lost, but worship is exclusively for the Body of Christ. The idea of *evangelistic worship* is a contradiction of terms.

Returning to the church conflict illustration, I found myself faced with a dilemma. The leadership requested that I only play songs that were familiar to people. I was to use a predictable formula of leading two fast songs, one moderate tempo song, and two slow, worshipful songs. The pastor felt that new people who were visiting the church were not able to relate to the intense, spirit-led worship which the church was accustomed. I was given a list of the top one-hundred worship songs and asked to use these songs for my selections. For lack of a better explanation, I was basically told that the current worship experience of the church was not a palatable flavor in which people could comfortably enjoy taking in as a small indulgence to achieve a feel-good experience. I remained leading for a few months more, but the more I attempted to lead, the more I felt as if I was being smothered by redundancy and regiment. God eventually released me from that particular ministry and reaffirmed my commitment to pursing genuine worship.

The answer to this wide-spread problem facing the modern day church can be easily rectified: move away from a *man-centered* worship focus and move towards a *God-centered* worship. Rather than asking: "How can we make the worship service more appealing to people?" we need to be asking ourselves: "How can we make our worship before the Lord more authentic, pure, and glorifying to Him?" It is critical to take seriously the Word of the Lord that reminds us:

> *I am the Lord; that is my name. I will not give my glory to another or my praise to idols* (Isaiah 42:7).

When the purpose of the worship service is particularly geared to be a bridge to allow unbelievers to experience worship in a non-threatening environment, what in reality, are we doing? We're focused on pleasing the world, glorifying our church and receiving praise from outsiders! We're striving to be the relevant church that has made a name for itself in the community because of the way we do church. This is not the prescribed formula found throughout scripture. The church in the first century was hated by the world. They didn't make the monotheistic worship of Christianity appeal to the polytheistic worship of the pagans. It wasn't their worship that drew the masses to come to Christ. It was the power of the Holy Spirit working through their lives that came as a result of their worship that enabled them to go into the world and evangelize.

In worship there is no common ground for believers and unbelievers to stand together in a unified cause of bringing glory to the Lord. 2 Corinthians 5 makes the analogy that we, as Christians, have been called to the ministry of reconciliation by being *"ambassadors"* of Christ to this world. This ministry is based upon the Christian being a representative of God's kingdom as he lives in the world. They are "in the world" but "not of the world." Paul's command in 2 Corinthians 6:14-18 tells the church that *"righteousness and wickedness"* and *"light and darkness"* have nothing in common. The church is to remain "separate" from the world and not to find common ground with unbelievers in the context of the Christian life experience. Central to the Christian's life and values, both corporately and individually, is worship. Because we have brought together what God has commanded us to separate, the genuine has become corrupted. The church cannot afford to compromise the holy and sacred for the sake of getting a stamp of approval from the world. If the church is to regain God's intended status of being His "ambassadors" and truly experience the benefits of being the "sons and daughters of God," then we must refrain from blending the participation of the holy and profane in worship.

Until we do so, we will continue to hunger for a genuine and authentic taste of worship. Perhaps it's time we discover that evangelical vanilla is one flavor of worship that adds no nutritional value to the spirit and leaves one famished for a taste of just one morsel of something real that will sustain the soul.

Chapter Two

Lessons from the Well

*Yet a time is coming and has now come when the
true worshipers will worship the Father in spirit
and in truth, for they are the kind of worshipers
that the Father seeks. God is spirit and his
worshipers must worship in spirit and in truth.*
John 4:23-24

The greatest hindrance of true worship is religion. While worship was created in the mind and heart of God, the origin of *religion* was fashioned through the darkness of men's hearts. Its beginnings are seen as far back as the Garden of Eden. As Adam and Eve made the choice to eat of the forbidden fruit from the tree of knowledge, it encapsulated the very essence of religion: man's interpretation of God's Word by man's standard in an attempt to meet man's needs.

All religion is based on some measure of truth. Adam and Eve chose a truth that offered them an idea of being *"like God, knowing good and evil"* (Genesis 3:5). In their minds they equated that being *"like God"* was to be equal to God. In Philippians 2:6 Paul's interesting point recognizes that Jesus, being the second Adam, *"did not consider equality with God something to be grasped."* Sin was not the only thing that entered the world when Adam and Eve made the choice to eat of the fruit. In one sense, they discovered that they could create something in the world which had never existed before. Based on a new found knowledge of good and evil, defined by their own standard of right and wrong, creation's first couple formed from their own image what has come to be known as *religion*.

Fast forward a few thousand years to a hot summer's day in the desert heat of Samaria. Life in first century Israel displayed various expressions of religious life. Not only were paganism and several forms of cult worship thriving, but even within the ranks of Judaism there were conflicting sects that interpreted the worship of Yahweh in drastically different ways. From Judaism came the Pharisees, Sadducees, and Essenes; however, often missed and most despised within this list were the Samaritans.

The Samaritans represented everything wrong with the idea of religion. They based their foundational worship practices on the Pentateuch, the first five books of the Old Testament. Conversely, the Samaritans also practiced syncretism by incorporating some of the surrounding pagan beliefs into their worship rituals. After the exile the Jews refused the Samaritans participation in building the temple in Jerusalem because they had become a defiled people through the intermarriage with pagan nations. In response, the Samaritans built their own temple on Mount Gerizim (the location where Moses gave the blessings over the children of Israel) and instituted their own priesthood. Tensions rose, battles raged and hatred separated a people who were linked eternally as brothers yet divided as fierce enemies. Ultimately, the conflict between the two people groups could be summed up as a war over worship.

On this particular day, a Samaritan was about to discover a truth about worship that would forever change her life. Enter the woman at the well: a lonely, rejected and immoral woman who knew the full meaning of the word *outcast*. Little did she know that her life would drastically change when she encountered the most unlikely of people—a Jewish man. To her surprise, the man who spoke to her did not fulfill the stereotypical expectations of what she had come to expect from a Jew. She could tell he possessed a prophetic gift by the way he was able to look into the depths of her heart by penetrating it with the words of truth. She suffered several failed marriages and now, once again, found herself involved in another relationship. Even more astonishing than the man's revelation of her failed sinful past and her current life of immorality, the stranger had made an admission that no one else would have dared to proclaim: like the Samaritan religion, Jewish worship had become an unacceptable form of worship.

Jesus explained to the woman that the Jews worship what they *do know* referring to the testimony of the Torah. Although its purpose was to guide God's chosen people along the path of acceptable worship to Yahweh, the Jews had failed to practice true worship. Jesus never challenged the spirit of the Torah when He spoke out against the religiousness of His day; instead, He challenged the lack of truth that resulted from a wrong interpretation of the Word of God. Jesus proclaimed to the Samaritan woman that a day would come when people would no longer worship at the temple in Jerusalem (John 4:21).For Jesus to allude to the idea that the temple worship in Jerusalem would one day be obsolete was blasphemy in the mind of a Jew. In fact, He would make it very clear that both the Samaritans and the Jews were missing something essential to worship—*spirit* and *truth.*

One has to wonder why Jesus chose the words *spirit and truth* to describe the essence of true worship. For Samaritans and Jews alike, worship encompassed the idea of rituals, places and appointed times. I can imagine, to the surprise of the woman, Jesus' statement concerning the need to no longer observe temple worship was shocking. Up to this point, she was excluded from worship with her people. She had no place in either world of Judaism or Samaritanism. Now, a prophet had come to tell her that those who had cast her out were outcasts as well.

The Greek word *pneuma,* from which we translate the word *spirit,* carries the basic meaning of "wind or air in motion." Wind is something we cannot fully comprehend; yet we are able to describe its presence, power and affect upon our world. If I were to ask someone to draw an image of wind (not trees blowing in the wind), I would be asking for an impossible thing. Wind can't be seen, yet its effects can be observed in both subtle and devastating ways (e.g. tornadoes and hurricanes). Additionally, one cannot even begin to find a place of origin for the wind. All that we know about wind is summed up in the words of Jesus:

The wind blows wherever it pleases. You hear its sound, but you cannot tell where it comes from or where it is going (John 3:8).

In the same manner, God cannot be fully explained which is the exact thing religion attempts to do. It strives to place God in a well-contained box and hold Him to the boundaries we create for Him. For the Jew, the boundary measured from temple worship to the Torah to the Oral tradition. For the Samaritan, the boundary was neatly contained in the Pentateuch, Mount Gerizim, and syncretistic compromises. But like the wind, God cannot be contained in the framework of man's ideas. In other words, man does not set the conditions for worship. God is Spirit and He cannot be contained through the forming of an image that fits comfortably into our religious or theological preference.

Oddly enough, as I am writing this portion of the book, it is an extremely windy day in Wisconsin. Blowing for several hours, the wind has steadily maintained gusts between twenty-five and forty miles per hour. As I look out the window of my friend's farmhouse (where I am enjoying a few hours of quiet), I can see that the trees are violently rocking back and forth in a continuous, chaotic-like rhythm. On this day, the "trees of the field" are doing more than simply "clapping their hands." Instead, they are dancing unashamedly before their Maker unplanned, unritualized, unorganized and untheologized in their choreography of praise. The trees are simply responding to the presence of the wind. There is nothing comfortable about the experience. What fascinates me even more is realizing all of the things which are not trees feeling the effects of the wind. The wind has not let up for the sake of comfort for the grass nor have the trees minimized their joyous expression in celebrating the wind's presence as to not disturb the leaves on the ground.

By now I believe you may be getting my point. When Jesus said the "true worshipers" will worship in "spirit," He was expressing the idea of something that cannot be contained in man's mind or the physical world. Worship transcends man and originates from God. Innate to every human is the capacity to worship. We, as humans, were created with the desire to glorify someone or something in the context of our lives. To the man that glorifies this world, all that he does speaks of his worship as he relentlessly pursues possessions, power and pleasure. It's not so much about how he pursues these things that makes the successful man of the world stand out, but it is the intangible drive that fuels his pursuit found at the heart of all he does.

In the same way, when a tree is being blown around by a strong wind, we might say, "Look at that tree," but in reality, we are saying, "Look at what the wind is doing to that tree." It is the force behind the tree which has caused the tree to respond. By no means does the tree cause the wind to blow. It does not devise a strategic plan to create an atmosphere where the conditions would be right for the wind to blow. It does not dictate to the wind the manner in how, when or where it will be moved. The wind blows and the tree moves accordingly! This is the spirit of worship. It is not about a religious reasoning that sets certain parameters in order to illicit a response from God, but rather it is God setting the parameters of the heart so man will respond to Him.

When Jesus arrived on the scene of the first century world this was the reasoning of Judaism. The mindset reflected the belief of: "If we do what the Law and Traditions of the Elders have set forth, then Yahweh will look upon us and respond with His blessing." It's the trees suggesting that by growing tall, keeping green leaves and producing strong roots they can make the wind blow. In reality, Jesus came to fulfill the days which the prophet Jeremiah and the prophet Ezekiel spoke of:

I will put my law in their minds and write it on their hearts (Jeremiah 31:33).

I will give them an undivided heart and put a new spirit in them. I will remove from them their heart of stone and give them a heart of flesh (Ezekiel 11:19).

11

Had the religious leaders of the day taken note of what the prophets proclaimed, they would have understood that worship was one day going to look much different than what they had been accustomed. It would be the same wind but it would be blowing much differently than it had before.

As for the Samaritans, they were waiting for the One whom Moses spoke of in Deuteronomy 18 reminding them that God would bring a *"prophet from among your own brothers"* (v.15). This prophet would speak the very words of God and the people would be accountable for the message he proclaimed. The problem, as Jesus pointed out, was that the Samaritans worshiped what they did not "know." Something essential was missing from their worship that was absolutely necessary for their worship to be accepted by God—truth!

The fatal flaw of Samaritan thought was that it had adopted the partial truth of God's Word and rejected the remainder of His Word. Like the Jews, the Samaritans shared much of the same heritage. They had gone through the same history and the same exile because they were the same people. They knew the words of Jeremiah, Isaiah and other prophets, but because they refused to obey the commands of the Lord in not intermarrying with the pagan nations, they sought to redefine God's Word. Because they only accepted the Pentateuch as being the Word of God, they became disconnected with the plan of God for His people. Their rejection of the words of the prophets meant that they had rejected truth. One might say this was an early picture of postmodern thought by adopting the philosophy: "I don't agree with your truth so I'll make up my own." The Samaritans worshiped what they did not "know" because their entire system of worship was not based on God's truth.

When we consider the world in which Jesus proclaimed that the *"true worshipers will worship the Father in spirit and in truth"* (John 4:23), we begin to understand the full impact of those words. To worship in "spirit" is to surrender one's life as a response to glorifying God. As A.W. Tozer notes, "We must learn that we cannot have our own way and worship God as we please."[1] He furthers this thought by explaining that it is "impossible for any of us to worship God without the impartation of the Holy Spirit."[2]

True worship functions on the level of the Spirit. If we choose our own ideas and rituals as a means to worship the Lord, we negate the aspect of spirit. When Jesus came He challenged those functions and offered Himself as the template in approaching worship. He fulfilled the imagery of the temple, the feasts of the Lord, and the priesthood. It is the Spirit of Christ that personifies worship and if the life of His Spirit is not personified in our lives it is impossible for us to be participants of true worship.

As I have alluded to before, I have a past that at times did not reflect the actions of a worshiper of the Lord. Several years ago, I bought in to a lie. I had a thriving ministry and by all appearances, I was successful at what I was doing. In leading worship and preaching messages, people actively responded to what God was doing through the gifts He had placed within me for His glory. The deception crept in as I believed my *giftings* validated my spirituality. As sin surfaced in my heart, I neglected to address the issue before the Lord. Instead, I assumed that it was not affecting my life in a significant way due to my ability to use my gifts effectively in ministry. God allowed this to carry on for a season until the delusion of believing that I could harbor sin and still maintain an anointing without consequence was exposed. Much like Samson in the Book of Judges, there came a point when God's hand of favor upon my life was removed and I was left with the devastating effects of my sin (Judges 16:20).

It should not surprise us when men with an anointing upon their ministries are suddenly destroyed by sin. When something like this happens, we often ask: "How can that be since they have the Holy Spirit validating the anointing upon their ministry?" In answering, we must first recognize that God's grace extends well beyond what we are able to conceive. If we're honest with ourselves, we will discover that God puts up with much more than He should when it comes to the messes we make in our lives; nonetheless, though His grace abounds we may eventually insult the spirit of grace and be forced to reckon with the consequences of His redeeming discipline. As a result of my own experience, I can testify that a *sin* problem is a result of a *truth* problem. When we ignore truth in our lives and in our worship of the Lord, we can be convinced to believe anything.

This explains why a person can be drawn to God through His Spirit and yet deny the truth of what they discover when they come into His presence. In fact, it can be ignored altogether. It is possible for people to gather together in the name of the Lord and experience something spiritual while at the same time remain miles away from Biblical truth. Mormonism, Buddhism, Hinduism and Islam all experience something spiritual in their worship observance; however, the spiritual reality they experience is not based upon God's truth. If that is the case for individuals who worship in a cult setting, what does it say about those who worship the Lord? Can a church become a place that is spiritually charged with people shouting praises, dancing in the aisles, crying out to the Lord with weeping and glorifying the Name of Jesus while still being in error to the truth? The church of Sardis provides insight to this thought:

> *I know your deeds; you have a reputation of being alive but you are dead . . . Remember therefore what you have received and heard; obey it, and repent* (Revelation 3:1-3).

What did they receive and hear? It was God's Word and God's truth. They had the reputation of being a church that was seen as passionate worshipers of Christ but the reality was (not their reality but God's) that they were *dead*.

God has set forth the standard of how worship is to be defined. We are not privileged to add or to take away from what He has deemed as being absolutely essential for genuine worship to take place. When truth is violated and we redefine that truth an entirely new standard of belief is adopted, and we come to accept it as my way of worshipping. This was true of the Samaritans and eventually became true for the Jews. When Judaism could no longer follow the obligations of worship set forth in the Old Testament because the temple was destroyed in 70 A.D., they redefined worship by opting to study the Torah as their means of fulfilling the requirements of the Law.

In worship, spirit empowers while truth validates. Spirit and truth must exist in equal measure and importance in worship.

If we error on the side of truth that is void of spirit, the result will be religious ritual. If we fail to observe truth and simply run with spirit, we end up with an emotionally fueled heresy or even worse the forming of a cult. And what is the lesson of the well? It is through Jesus Christ that both the spirit and truth are given. He alone is the personification of true worship and when we accept the life of Christ as our own we become what God desires for each of us: to be true worshipers who worship the Father in spirit and in truth.

The idea of *spirit* speaks to the fact that worship is something beyond an intellectual ascent or an emotional experience. It is something that encounters the whole of God and envelopes the whole of man. Andrew Hill suggests, "True worship takes place on the inside, in the heart or spirit of the worshiper . . . it involves opening ourselves to the dangerous life of the Spirit."[3] Thus, worship is a relationship-based event that takes place between God and man which is initiated by the work of the Spirit. Without the intervention of the Spirit of God, man is unable to worship God. The idea of *truth* describes the revealed knowledge about God in His Word. Worship that is acceptable must be based upon the truth contained within Scripture. John MacArthur contests that true worship can only take place when one comes to "grips with the depth of spiritual truth . . . people can only rise high in worship in the same proportion" to which they have come to know in the "truths of the Word."[4] To worship in truth is to respond to the God revealed in Scripture by making one's life a product of what He commands and requires. Therefore, foundationally, worship must be Biblically established, Christ-centered and Spirit inspired. Any other attempt to worship God will vainly fail and produce a religion that can never satisfy the longing of a thirsty soul.

In my own journey, I have learned the lessons from the well. Like the Samaritan woman who was living in the wilderness of isolation due to the consequences of her sin, I have come to discover that true worship refreshes and restores the soul. It opens our eyes to the truth of God and it connects our spirit with His. Our own efforts, our own ideas and our own ways will forever leave us parched longing to have our thirst quenched.

Jesus offers spirit and truth as the only remedy for those longing to be satisfied in worshiping the Father. Drink from the spring of living water and discover:

Only You can fill this thirsting of my soul
Jesus You're the One my heart is longing for
Take me to the stream where the Living Water flows
Only You, You're all I need.
(from *Only You* by Jay T. Walls)

Chapter Three

God is Not Your Friend

'Woe to me!' I cried. 'I am ruined . . .'
Isaiah 6:5

When I saw him, I fell at his feet as though dead.
Revelation 1:17

As I sit in a crowded Starbucks, I vividly remember my days as a manager for one of their stores on the east side of Milwaukee. This location was known for its diverse culture; therefore, I encountered many interesting people who proudly portrayed their beliefs in their conversations, opinions and even their wardrobe. One young man, who we'll call "Joe," comes to mind as I reflect upon my days at the coffee shop.

Joe typified the average film student attending a liberal college. He was witty, opinionated, artistic and shared a passion for social concerns. Although I cannot recall any specifics of our conversations, I can still remember the day when he came into the store wearing a brown t-shirt with a picture of Jesus on the front. I gave a slight chuckle when I read the words "Jesus is my homeboy" written across the front. I'm not sure where Joe's heart was in regards to his salvation, but in observing his words and actions it was evident that the fruits of his life were not conducive to godly living. As I think back on that t-shirt, I do not find it as humorous as I once did. I believe that the statement

"Jesus is my homeboy" epitomizes everything wrong with the experience of modern day worship.

Is Jesus our homeboy? My perspective was radically changed one day when I read this quote by scholar D.A. Carson: "not once is Jesus or God ever described in the Bible as our friend."[5] At first, I was somewhat taken back by that thought. "Surely God is my friend!" I argued, "After all, the Bible tells me *'He is a friend that sticks closer than a brother.'*" In actuality, I discovered that Proverbs 18:24 states:

> *"A man of many companions will come to ruin, but there is a friend that sticks closer than a brother."*

Contextually, this verse is not referring to God but to the fact that our relationships with one another should not be carelessly based on superficial friendships. A man will come to "ruin" if he only pursues relationships to merely have friends rather than seeking relationships that develop accountability, wisdom, trust and honesty. Nowhere in Scripture do we read where someone called God their friend. There are, however, instances where God calls us "friend" as seen in the accounts of Abraham being a "friend of God" and Jesus calling the Twelve "His friends."

You might be wondering at this point, "What's the big deal? What harm is there in thinking that God is my friend? After all, that's how I relate to Him." I wholeheartedly believe this ideology is one of the major problems within the church today. A few years ago, theologian David Wells wrote a book entitled *God in the Wasteland.* Written in 1994, Wells shared his concern for the condition of the Evangelical church in regards to how they had begun viewing God, and he reflected upon the possible outcomes if that trend continued. Almost prophetically, it seems as if Wells' thoughts are applicable for what we are seeing today in the area of worship:

> The consequence of all this is that was once transcendent in the doctrine of God has either faded or been relocated to the category of the immanent, and then this diminished God has been

further reinterpreted to accommodate modern needs. These alterations have drastically changed the whole meaning of Christian faith. They have affected the way we view God in relation to ourselves, to life and to history. They affect the way we think of his love, his goodness, his saving intentions, what his salvation means, how he reveals himself, how his revelation is received, why Christ was incarnated, and what significance this has for other religions.[6]

Wells observed a shift in the way that the church culture began to view God. For years God was seen as someone who was unapproachable in His holiness, majesty and splendor. Historically, Catholicism and Greek Orthodox championed this thought by epitomizing this picture of the transcendent God within the cultural mindset. This overemphasis caused many to have a distorted view of man's ability to relate to God. Being far too holy and awesome, God was to be feared and worshiped at a distance.

The transcendence of God refers to the idea that He is "wholly other" and is "exalted far above the created universe" making Him unfathomable.[7] Failure to recognize this attribute of God results in worship that attempts to bring God down to the level of man.[8] Truths such as the holiness of God, the fear of God and the wonder of God are diminished for the sake of approaching God as friend rather than One who lives in *"unapproachable light"* (1 Timothy 6:16).[9] Our causal and comfortable worship setting on Sunday mornings which often includes a complete coffee service, dressed down attire, lingering fellowship and a dire need to read the *word of the bulletin* while God is being honored, speaks to our lack of understanding of God's transcendence (in and of themselves aren't necessarily wrong). If we truly thought of God as being holy, majestic, awesome, powerful and unapproachable as the Bible describes Him, I would almost guarantee that Sunday mornings would consist of believers seen on their faces *sucking carpet* before God rather than sipping *Starbucks* in order to stay awake for the service!

Two of the most vivid portraits of men who caught a glimpse of the transcendence of God are found in the accounts of the prophet Isaiah's vision (Isaiah 6) and the Apostle John's vision (Revelation 1). For both, seeing the transcendence of God was anything but a causal experience. Had they been sipping a hot cup of coffee while sitting in a church pew during this encounter, I shudder to think of the potential *McDonalds* type of lawsuits that would have resulted due to hot java being thrown upon the congregants. Perhaps this is why God isn't showing up in our services as we have created a hazardous worship environment in the sanctuary! I cannot imagine Isaiah or John with coffee in hand crying out "Jesus! You're my homeboy and I praise you!" Yet how often do we portray this in our actions when we come into the presence of the Lord?

In the 1980's a new emphasis of worship music began to infiltrate the mainstream church worship setting. Initially, *Maranatha Music* had produced a more intimate-based song style compared to the high-praise, energetic and fully orchestrated songs of *Hosanna/Integrity Music.* However, the landscape of church music would forever be changed as the Vineyard church introduced music that seemed to be unprecedented in capturing the Father's heart and in promoting a unique sense of intimacy in worship. To be quite honest, when I first heard music from the *Vineyard*, I thought it was weird! In my mind, I pictured flower children dancing among fields of dandelions without a care in the world. The truth of the matter is that I could not relate to the depth of intimacy being presented through the music and lyrics. As I exposed myself to more of this approach to worship, I quickly moved away from my Catholic roots of seeing God as the One I was to fear and I gravitated towards the idea of a loving Father who wanted nothing more than for me to get to know Him in a special way.

Before we proceed, I want to assure you that I believe that knowing God personally and intimately should be the life goal of every true worshiper. We cannot truly experience the fullness that the life of worship brings to us without intimacy with Christ. Great caution must be observed in our attempts to know God. We can alter our perception of Him for the sake of remaining comfortable in the relationship. I am grateful for what the *Vineyard* music movement has contributed to my development as a worshiper. Many of the musicians have labored in order to bring the Body of Christ together in pursuing a deeper and more meaningful worship experience. They have truly taught us how to capture the heart of the Father in worship.

The quest for deeper intimacy in striving to know God has fueled a passion to experience God on an extremely personal level. The problem, nonetheless, goes beyond the music and lyrics. The pendulum which was unbalanced on the side of God's transcendence has now moved to the other side. The pendulum swing has generated a misguided emphasis of God's love, grace and mercy while diminishing His justice, discipline and wrath. God no longer stands as the Creator of every living thing who is to be feared in reverence and awe; rather, He has become a God who sympathizes with our sin, failure and inability to live holy as His "grace is enough" and His only desire is to "draw me close" to Himself. The result has yielded a causal approach to the Creator of the Universe making our friendship with Christ the basis of our worship.

Most of us have heard the old adage, "familiarity breeds contempt." Unfortunately, this saying is a crystal clear picture of worship in the church today. Something is lost in a relationship when we no longer see the other person in light of who they really are. The danger of familiarity is in losing a sense of respect and becoming too casual toward another in regard to their role, purpose and significance in our life. If this tendency is not corrected, we will come to a point where we no longer value what the other person deems as essential to the relationship.

Have you ever wondered why it appears that we no longer have a respect for God in our country? We might blame this on the increase of wickedness in these last days; but what if this is due to the church's general attitude toward God? Seldom can you walk into any given church in America on any given Sunday and come out saying, "I have experienced the fear of God today!" Instead, we say things like "That was a great sermon" or "The worship was awesome." In other cases we may say "I could barely stay awake because the pastor was so boring" or "The worship team needs serious help!" We have all been guilty at one time or another in leaving a service with less than godly thoughts. In fact, I believe there are times when we leave church acting more fleshy than spiritual. How often do we walk away from a service feeling as if we are ungrateful, undeserving, undisciplined, unholy, unable and unimportant for being in God's presence? When was the last time we caught a glimpse of ourselves as being selfish, self-absorbed, self-gratifying and self-centered worms of a people because we have seen ourselves in light of a holy, awesome and unapproachable God? My experience tells me it's not too often enough!

Contrary to popular teachings such as: *Your Best Life Now, The Purpose Driven Life,* and *Love Wins,* there is a side of us that should feel completely unworthy and undeserving of anything when we think about the transcendence of God. We have reduced our God to someone who is so wrapped up in the personal affairs of our lives that His sole desire is to make our lives successful in this world. This attitude has developed because we have assumed that in our familiarity with God, He wants us to be happy. After all, this is what friends do for each other. They bring pleasure to our lives as we experience life together. How often do we say to our friends, "I can't wait for the day when your spouse dies so that I can be there to comfort you?" No, our desire is to experience life's good times with our friends. Difficult times will certainly occur in our relationships, but if we had our way, we would go to great lengths to avoid anything that would threaten our happiness together. If we insert Jesus into this mindset, what purpose does He serve for us? Wouldn't it be great to have a friend you could offend on an ongoing basis; you could ignore him when convenient; he would even cover the expense for all of your mistakes and you would never have to pay him back. Oh, and by the way, you would be free of all guilt and shame for causing his pain and suffering. This is the American Jesus whom we have come to adore and have been privileged to call our "friend!"

When confronted with a holy and awesome God, the accounts of Isaiah's and John's reactions are powerful. By the American Christian standards of today, these men are spiritual giants. Isaiah was a prophet of the Lord. Most scholars believe that his "vision" was not his first and he was most likely an established prophet in Judah before the occurrence of Isaiah 6. He was a man who walked closely with the Lord and was given access to the intimate thoughts of God's heart. And yet when he saw the Lord he became so overwhelmed with dread that he thought he was going to die!

Like Isaiah, John was also a privileged individual in this life. In fact, there was not a person on the face of the earth who held a closer and more personal relationship with Jesus while He walked on the earth. Certainly, John knew the heart of Jesus. As far as friendship, John had experienced the Lord's closeness like no one else in his day. On one Sunday morning, this Jesus who John knew so well suddenly revealed Himself in majesty and glory and John fell down as though he was dead! I am willing to go out on a limb and submit with one hundred percent of certainty that during these encounters neither man entertained the notion of "God, You're my best friend!"

I can understand the idea behind considering God as our friend in that it is difficult to find a proper frame of reference in describing our relationship with Him. What we need to keep in mind is that God supersedes the idea of friend. He is not One who walks through life on common ground with us. Jesus experienced the journey of humanity, and He shares in our humanity—but He is much more than someone who can be assigned to the designation of friend in our lives. How many friends can say to me, *"I knew you before you were formed in the womb"* (Psalm 139:13-16)? To how many of our friends can we say, *"Where can I go from your Spirit? Where can I flee from your presence"* (Psalm 139:7)? *Friend* is simply too common of an idea to assign to our relationship with God. It reduces Him to someone that fits comfortably within our thoughts without making us feel too uneasy about the reality of who He is.

The end result in adopting the view of *God is my friend* is a lack of holiness. God becomes just another friend in a long list of our friends and acquaintances, and we often pretend that He is at that top of that list. In our culture, friendship carries the idea that if a person is my friend, he will accept me no matter what I do, say or believe. For those we allocate as our best friends, we assume that they accept the good, bad and ugly of our lives. But in all of this, have we considered who God truly is? David Wells articulates this description of the transcendent God:

> Scripture indicates that there are two aspects of the outside God's transcendence. On the one hand, God is transcendent because he is self-sufficient, owing nothing to creation for his own life, and so powerful that he can always act within that creation. He is dependent on nothing outside of himself for the realization of his will but, because the creation is always and at every moment dependent upon him, he is always over it. On the other hand, he is transcendent because his utter moral purity separates him from all of human life and defines him in his essential character.[10]

When we fail to recognize that God is altogether unlike us in His nature, power and Person, we begin to cross the line of profaning Him. More than the modern day belief that *profanity* is profaning God, to profane God is to make God common. Holiness carries the idea that it is "separated or sacred." It is something that is "set apart". By virtue of who He is, God is set apart from all of Creation. When we attempt to bring Him into our world and view Him through our thoughts and beliefs rather than accept Him on what He has revealed of Himself to creation, we make the transcendent God nothing more than a product of our own imagination—and that is profaning Him!

In order for us to recapture a true picture of His transcendence, we need to once again behold a vision of His holiness. A.W. Tozer describes our difficulty of obtaining this vision due to an "unwillingness to take God as He is and to adjust our lives accordingly" because we continually attempt to "modify Him and bring Him nearer to our own image."[11] If we only desire to see God as the One who draws near to us on earth, then we will miss the heavenly aspects of His Person. To only see Him as a Savior who loved us enough to die on a cross to be our friend, will restrict us from experiencing the glory of a resurrected Lord who will give us the keys to a kingdom that is "not of this world." If we, however, allow ourselves to approach God with unveiled eyes and open hearts, I believe we will see what God longs to show His people. Like the prophet Isaiah and Apostle John, heaven will open up and God will reveal Himself to His people. The church will rise up to fulfill its purpose and God's kingdom will be demonstrated with power through the body of Christ. And if that can happen, the world we live in will once again know of the glory of God through those who worship Him in spirit and in truth.

Chapter Four

I Am a Friend of God

Come near to God and He will come near to you.
James 4:8

You are my friends if you do what I command . . .
I have called you friends, for everything that I
learned from my Father I have made known to you.
John 15:14-15

Although there is a need to recapture the worship of the transcendent God, the importance of knowing the imminent God must not be understated. Christianity offers what no other religion can claim: the Creator of the Universe is a God who desires to be personally intimate with His creation. Rather than using worship as a means to appease God, worship, for the Christian, is an act of intimacy that promotes a deeper relationship with God. The problem is not that the church has lacked the passion to know God intimately, but that the church has misunderstood what intimacy with the imminent God actually implies.

Classically, the imminence of God refers to the nearness of God to man and God's interaction with His creation. While this definition can give us a general understanding of imminence, it can also be problematic. For instance, if I were to ask ten different believers to explain what the *nearness of God to man* means, I would most certainly get ten different answers. Because of the adoption of postmodern thinking in today's church culture, the response to the question would likely reflect a phrase such as, "For me, it means . . ." This is not necessarily a wrong answer, but it is a dangerous one as it can potentially promote the worship of a personal God who is defined by the person and not God.

If you were to go back several centuries, the idea of an imminent God would have been a foreign if not a heretical thought. The rise of Catholicism in the fifth and sixth centuries brought with it a new emphasis on the worship experience. Before that point in history, the early church enjoyed a simplistic worship that stressed intimacy, reverence and heartfelt expressions centered on the message of the Gospel. As the church became more powerful under the rule of Constantine and made the official religion of the Roman Empire, the dynamic of church worship changed. Symbols, relics, rituals and rites permeated the landscape of Christian worship. Worship shifted from the humble gatherings of simplistic meetings to events of pomp and circumstance that endeavored to evoke a response of awe toward an unreachable God. As the Catholic church progressed, worship became a non-participatory activity for the laity. Those who filled the church pews were sometimes at the mercy of corrupt priests who, in the people's minds, were the only connection between man and God. In essence, God became so far removed in the eyes of the common man that worship was nothing more than acknowledging God as the unfathomable, unattainable and unrelateable Creator.

After the Reformation the church was awakened to the idea that God desires a personal relationship with His creation. New emphasis on Scripture, doctrine and personal piety began to shape the way in which people approached their worship practices. This resulted in a variety of worship expressions in the Body of Christ that ultimately shaped the portrait of mainline Protestant, Evangelical, Charismatic and Pentecostal denominations.

Although the above mentioned is an abbreviated summary of the development of Christian worship over the last two thousand years, the point is that for several hundred years the church has been developing and continues to develop its own theology to answer the question of "How do we get closer to

God?" The transformation of worship that took place in the latter half of the twentieth century has verified the trend toward the imminent God. Many churches have made great strides to shy away from anything that resembles a religious view of God such as terminologies and traditions. Instead, their focus has been placed upon presenting a God whose sole concern is in a personal, mutual relationship with His people. Today's mindset has further developed the idea of God's imminence. For instance, in speaking of salvation, we ask if people would like to receive Jesus as their *personal Savior*—a term that the Bible never uses. This is furthered in many of today's churches as Jesus is not only seen as sympathizing with our weaknesses but also embraces our humanity in accepting our failure and sin.

While many believe that today's worship experience brings us to a place of encountering the imminent God, my concern for the church is that, in truth, we may not be experiencing the imminent God at all. Could it be that the God we aim to know so intimately is one that has been fashioned in our minds rather than through the truth of Scripture? If we consider for a moment the transcendence of God, we will discover that His other-worldly nature is not without a redemptive purpose in our lives. His invisible qualities are something that should draw us nearer to Him (Romans 1:20). As James 4:8 states, *"Come near to God and he will come near to you."* Inferred in these Scriptures is the idea of a distance that exists between God and man. This is God's transcendence. It is His incomparable divine nature that man—even redeemed man—will never come to know. And yet through Christ, God has found a way to bridge this canyon between two worlds.

I am a firm believer that we cannot come to Christ without first seeing Him as the transcendent God. We do not put our faith in a Savior with the thought of "He's just like me." The contrary is true. We put our faith in Christ for salvation because we have come to recognize the irreconcilable distance that separates us from our Creator. Needless to say, it is God's transcendence that leads us to His imminence. Although the church of the past erred in creating a transcendent God who was not seen as being imminent, except through the mediation of a chain of *spiritually perfected* individuals (i.e. the priesthood, saints, Mary, etc . . .), the result still drew people to discovering a closer and deeper experience with God.

Today's worship experience focuses upon the believer's privilege of having *"confidence to enter the Most Holy Place"* (Hebrews 10:19) and meeting with God "face to face." I, for one, never want to take this privilege for granted; however, I question if we have truly participated in this given freedom which allows us to closely behold the Almighty God in worship. In some ways, worship can be seen as being the activity of man attempting to draw close to God; as a result, God will draw near to man. During this experience an incredible exchange takes place which is too often overlooked: an exchange of God's glory and man's glory.

Because God is a God of glory, we cannot escape the reality that He is present in our world. The Hebrew word *kabod,* where we derive our translation *glory,* communicates the idea of weightiness. In speaking of God's glory, we are in essence speaking of the full weight of all that exudes from His presence and is pressed upon all of which He has created. Man is also given glory by the Lord, although it is flawed and fleeting. 1 Peter 1:24 states, *"All men are like grass and all of their GLORY [emphasis added] is like the flowers of the field"* and 1 Corinthians 11:7 speaks of women being the "glory of man."

True worship encompasses the idea that man, in all of his glory, willingly places the full weight of his entire being at the feet of His Creator. In return, God then places His glory, the weight of His presence, upon and within man. A mysterious and unfathomable exchange happens. Worship is more than just religious ritual or an exchange of friendship. It is an organic process ever expanding in the heart of man from the heart of God. This experience defines the imminence of God in the worship setting.

If we once again consider the stories of Isaiah and the Apostle John, we can see similarities in their response to the glory of God. Their visions reveal a picture of the transcendent God who came imminently near them. Isaiah became "undone" and John "fell at His feet as though dead!" It wasn't because they simply considered how holy and awesome God was but because the Holy and Awesome God came near to them. There wasn't a response of over-hyped celebration; a simple applause; amen, praise the Lord; or thank-you, Jesus, uttered under their breath. No, these men were completely humbled and aware of the fact that they did not belong in the presence of the Lord. They became keenly aware of their humanity and overwhelmed with the thought of God's holiness. The full weight of their glory was crushed under the weight of God's presence. And in that moment, neither one would dare to allow one ounce of their fleshy human nature to surface in the midst of their worship.

It's time to ask some honest questions. Does this describe the worship experience of the church today? Have we become so overwhelmed with the glory of God that we respond the same way? I know what many of you are thinking: "These were isolated and special times in which the Lord visits His people in an uncommon way." Again, I'm not sure that Scripture even promotes this sort of thinking. I would be more apt to ask: "Why doesn't God visit us more this way in our worship experience?" The answer is in our unwillingness to give up our glory for the sake of obtaining His and this boils down to one fatal flaw of today's church: disobedience!

Have we ever stopped to realize that God is as near to us as He can possibly be? God ensured a way for us to discover Him as being the imminent God. John 1:14 states, *"The Word became flesh and made His dwelling among us."* Jesus became the external picture of God's presence surrounding humanity; yet God made His imminence in our lives even more present. 1 Corinthians 3:16 and 6:19 remind us that we are the *"temple of the Holy Spirit"* and that His Spirit lives in us. Now, God's Spirit not only dwells among us but He also dwells in us. How much closer can God be? His glory is in us and should be seen through us! (2 Corinthians 3:16-18).

When people see your life, what do they see? Do they feel the weight of you or does the weight of God permeate your entire being? Is there an instant sense from others that God is in their midst when they are in your presence? Go back and read the book of Acts. It's amazing when you read it with this thought in mind. People were so convinced that God was present in the lives of the disciples that they even brought the sick to lay in the streets so that *"at least Peter's shadow might fall on them as he passed* by" (Acts 5:15). Is this the case in the modern day church? If not, we need to ask ourselves, "Why not?"

On the night He was betrayed, Jesus told the disciples:

> *You are my friends if you do what I command . . .*
> *I have called you friends, for everything that I*
> *learned from my Father I have made known to you*
> (John 15:14-15).

I don't believe that any one of us would dispute the fact that when people came in contact with Jesus, there was a definite sense of God's presence in their midst. This was the very thing which He learned from His Father and He exemplified for His disciples. Jesus lived a life of giving up His glory for the sake of obtaining God's glory. In John 15:14-15, Jesus describes the *how* of living in the same manner. In order to be truly identified with Christ, we must obtain intimacy with Christ. Without intimacy there will be no evidence of God's presence in our lives. Jesus makes this idea plain and simple: I will make myself close to you IF you *"obey what I have commanded"* (John 15:10). The evidence of our Christian faith—that God is in us—is fostered through obedience.

In principle there are only two commands that Jesus asks us to obey: *"Love the Lord your God with all your heart and with all your soul and with all your mind . . . And the second is like it: Love your neighbor as yourself"* (Matthew 22:37-39). This is how we show we are friends of God. This is the proof that God chooses to make Himself closely identified with us. Are we actually portraying obedience to these commands in our modern day worship setting? Do we fill our lives with choices and preferences that reflect obedient service to the Lord? Are our beliefs based on what we believe or what the Bible actually says? Say what we want, but the church in general is so consumer orientated that we base where, how, when and why we worship upon our likes and dislikes rather than out of complete obedience to the Lord. If we don't like the worship band, preacher, building, youth programs or whatever else rubs us the wrong way, we simply go somewhere else where our desires can be met. We even base the effectiveness of a worship service upon how it makes us feel.

Today's church excels in promoting the glory of man. We set up entire church structures and theologies that appeal to attendance in a church rather than the glory of God. We discuss in Sunday school classes how we can make fornicators, homosexuals, spouse abusers, child molesters, prostitutes and even atheists feel included and comfortable in the church and somehow hope that our love will win them to the kingdom. Yet, I am perplexed. If the man who walked closest to Jesus, while on earth, fell down as though "dead" when Jesus revealed His presence to him, how would those living in sin respond if the transcendent God suddenly became imminent in our midst? If there are times when we feel unworthy (even though we know we can boldly come before God's throne), why attempt to make sinners feel worthy to sit before a Holy and Awesome God? Review the Gospel accounts. Whenever Jesus confronted sinners in His love, their responses reflected a posture of unworthiness. He didn't condemn them and nor should we; however, He didn't cover up the glory of God within Him in order to make the sinner feel as if they were worthy of the presence of God.

If we are truly experiencing the imminence of God in today's church, a seeker-sensitive or emergent theology is a contradiction to the reality of what God's nearness should produce in our lives. As these teachings promote Jesus as *friend* and largely ignore Jesus as *Lord*, it is impossible to experience a God who is close without realizing how much we do not belong in His presence. The closer we come toward Him the more conviction surfaces within our hearts. He is perfect; we are not, and without Jesus Christ at the center of our lives we should be very uncomfortable. Minimalizing our unworthiness in comparison to God's worthiness cannot exist together when the glory of God meets the glory of man.

Something interesting happens to us when we have sin in our lives and ignore the conviction that comes upon us when being in the presence of the Lord. There was a time in my life when I harbored sin in my heart and conducted worship services where the richness of God's glory was present. I knew that God loved me and I believed that because of the experiences I had during the worship services God was content with me working through my issues. It felt great to be in His presence; however, I still felt miserable when the services were over. Back and forth I would go—enjoying the wonderful presence of God and then wailing in the misery of my sin. As long as I was leading worship all was fine. I knew that my *friend* was pleased to have me worship Him. Looking back, I realized my choice to be comforted in His love, mercy and grace while ignoring His still, small voice that echoed as it called out the sin in my heart amounted to nothing more than proving that I was not a friend of God. Unlike a true friend, I was using God.

The truth is that the church is guilty of not fully obeying the Lord. Because of this, God's glory cannot be seen through the lives of His people. Disobedience contradicts God's imminence to the world that surrounds the church. We have failed to be "friends of God" and live as Jesus lived in strict obedience to the Father. God will call us friends WHEN we walk with Him in obedience. What is the evidence of a people who claim that they "draw near to God" and He "draws near" to them? It is a people who are grafted into the vine and intimately joined with the Lord. This produces only one kind of fruit from such a relationship: obedience. Otherwise, we're simply living in a world in which we're pretending that God's glory fills our churches; when in reality, we are worshiping a God who makes us comfortable to bask in our own glory and suit our selfish needs.

Chapter Five

Satan's Dirty Little Secret

You were anointed as guardian cherub, for so I
ordained you. You were on the Holy Mount of God;
you walked among the fiery stones.
Ezekiel 28:14

All of your pomp has been brought down to
the grave, along with the noise of your harps . . .
How you have fallen from heaven, O morning star,
son of the dawn. You have been cast down to
the earth . . .
Isaiah 14:11-12

They say that everyone has a secret. It shouldn't surprise us to discover that a person we know or know of has a secret that when uncovered sends a shock wave of frenzy throughout society. Consider a man like Ted Bundy. Although I will refrain from all of the gruesome details of his sin, his story remains one of the most intriguing crime sagas in history. From all appearances, Bundy was a well-liked and successful career driven man. He held several job positions including being involved in the Republican Party political campaigns. Bundy even endeavored to pursue a law degree for which he received glowing recommendations from Governor Daniel Evans, Washington State Republican Party Chairman Ross Davis, and several of his former college psychology professors. And yet Ted Bundy had a terrible secret: He was a serial-killer. Bundy would later confess before his execution on January 24, 1989, that he had brutally killed thirty women; but as law enforcement officials began to gather additional evidence, it is probable that Bundy murdered many more.

Imagine how different things would have turned out for Bundy's victims if they had known of his dark secret. Had they been able to recognize what lay behind the façade of this charismatic and handsome man, they would still be experiencing the pleasures of this life. This short synopsis of one of America's most notorious serial-killers should remind us that not only are there people in this world who are capable of hiding such secrets which take the lives of many, but also that in the realm of the spirit, there is a more dangerous enemy who is more than capable of hiding his *dirty little secret* that is destroying the lives of millions of people.

In order to discover this secret that the enemy holds, we must go back to a time before man inhabited the earth. His secret originated in the heavenlies before man even uttered a single word of praise unto the Lord. Believe it or not, Satan, then called Lucifer, once resided in heaven. Making his story even more enthralling, Satan's residence in heaven placed him in a special role among all that God had created. In a general perspective held by many scholars, it is believed that the Archangel Lucifer was not only an angelic being, but also a being that embodied musical instruments for the purpose of heavenly worship unto the Lord. In Isaiah 14:11-12, the prophet makes a comparison between the King of Babylon and Lucifer. As Isaiah foretells of the inevitable fall of Babylon, he parallels it with the story of Lucifer and his damning fall from the heavenlies by describing him as being identified with music in saying "the noise of your harps."

Whether or not Isaiah is making a poetic analogy or has been given literal insight into the being of Lucifer, we are certain as to why Satan was cast out of heaven—it was over the issue of worship! The belief of Satan being the worship leader in heaven is somewhat speculative but it doesn't change the nature of his dirty little secret. Before I reveal that secret, I want to address a theological issue that troubles many of us concerning both the fall of Satan from heaven and the fall of man from the Garden.

Many of us struggle with the question of "How Satan could have sinned in heaven and how man could have sinned in the Garden of Eden?" I admit I struggled over the implications of these two events; however, there is an important insight that we seldom ever consider. In his book, *The Handbook for Spiritual Warfare,* Dr. Ed Murphy offers a sound explanation giving us a critical understanding on this subject. He states:

> All creatures are imperfect, however. By the very definition God cannot create God. He can only create beings which are less than God, and therefore, imperfect. His creation can never be equal to the Creator. By the very act of creating creatures in His own image and likeness, God is creating creatures with mind, emotions, and a will similar to His own. By definition He cannot create creatures in His own image and likeness which are not free to think, feel, and choose for themselves.[12]

All of God's creation was created good in the sense that we were recipients of the image of God and designed as He intended us to be. By design we were created with the capacity to exercise free will. At one time angels also shared in this ability. Despite the fact that Satan enjoyed the perfect atmosphere of heaven in the presence of a perfect God, he could never be fully like God and because of that there still remained a part of him that was imperfect. Had Satan been a perfect being, what would have driven him to the thought of seeing God has being more perfect than Him? After all, this is what Isaiah describes as being the issue in Satan's fall—he wanted to be God! The same holds true for Adam and Eve. If they had thought they were perfect then why did they want to become like God? (Genesis 3:5).

This brings us to discovering the truth of Satan's dirty little secret. Contrary to popular belief, the church is not the expert on the subject of worship. Long before we arrived on the scene, Satan was standing on the stage as the worship leader in heaven. If there is one created being that inhabits this earth who understands every aspect and nuance of true worship it is Satan. The cat is now out of the bag. The archenemy of our souls, the devil, knows more about the subject of worship than any of us can possibly know on this side of heaven. He knows how music, emotions, mind, will and spirit interact to produce an unadulterated product of pure worship before the throne of God. And this explains why he so vehemently and effectively opposes it.

Several years ago, I heard youth evangelist Reggie Dobbs preach a message on why Satan hates man so much and I have never forgotten it. He vividly explained the world in which Satan once lived as he worshiped in the heavenlies. Satan stood in a special place where he was privileged to worship before the face of God. Yet he was cast from heaven because of his pride and removed from that place of worship. God, in His Sovereign wisdom, gave this privilege to someone else. He created a being that had the capacity to inhabit His Spirit and to willfully and freely choose to stand in the place of worship where Satan once stood. God created the sanctuary for this being which he called the "Garden of Eden." God would create a perfect place where He would choose to dwell with this being, and in turn this being would choose to stand in His presence and worship his Creator face to face. Thus, God created humanity as the pinnacle of all He would ever create.

We can now have a more insightful picture of why the enemy was driven to sabotage all of mankind in the Garden. The aim of his existence has never changed. He will relentlessly do whatever he can in his power to ensure that man never stands in the place where he once stood. He will do whatever is necessary to pervert the essence of true worship and make worshippers bow down to anything other than the One who is truly worthy of our worship. Tozer notes that Satan carries an "ancient animosity" that drives him to seek an "unlimited dominion over the human family" and whenever his "evil ambition is challenged by the Spirit of God, he invariably retaliates with savage fury."[13]

38

We seldom think about the fact that while we are relishing in the presence of the Lord in our times of worship, Satan is unleashing an all-out war against us. Is it no wonder why one of the most predominate reasons that the Body of Christ experiences division is over worship in the church? Sure, we may not like the loud music, style of music, lack of hymns, failure to have weekly communion, having prayer at the end of service, or the pastor's sermon; but, who is actually fueling the fire of our attitudes and opinions that keeps the Body of Christ from joining together in unity to worship the Lord? The problem is not the worship ministry. The problem is that we are listening to the enemy's voice concerning the experience of worship.

In His infinite wisdom, God has given us all a place of worship. I'm not talking about a location or a certain time in which we escape this world and spend time with the Lord. No, I am speaking about a position which we are to maintain as one living the life of a worshipper. The Westminster Catechism describes this position in a simple yet profound way: "The chief end of man is to glorify God and enjoy Him forever." Our place of worship is a place where we position ourselves to be actively aware and participating in our supreme objective of glorifying God in all aspects of life.

The English word *glorify* is defined as "to make more glorious, to make more splendid, adorn, to extol, and to cause to seem more splendid or imposing than reality." By contrast, the word *usurp* means "to seize and hold (the power and the rights of another) without legal authority." If we are to live free of being deceived by Satan's dirty little secret then we will need to have a greater understanding of what these two words mean in regards to the life of worship.

Classically, we attribute the sin of pride to the demise of Satan in heaven, and while that is true, we also need to realize that pride takes on several different forms. Each must be recognized for its own unique danger posed to the Christian. It wasn't that pride had merely come into Satan's heart and then he was cast from heaven for thinking too highly of himself. It was the fact that Satan had a plan which revealed the worst kind of pride and still remains especially contagious to the human race—the usurping of the authority of God.

One of the more popular excuses used by believers who have no desire to pursue a deeper walk with the Lord is that they are only *human*. Gloating in the weakness of one's humanity is often worn as a badge to advocate a life of compromise and apathy. Although they intend to submit to the idea that as humans we all have weaknesses and perfection is beyond our ability, in reality, they are saying, "There is a part of my life which I glorify God and a part of my life which I glorify myself." Unfortunately, they fail to recognize that God did not create us for the benefit of pleasing ourselves. He did not create us to indulge ourselves in His blessing and then nominally give Him the glory and honor due His Name. And yet we pretend that there are parts of our lives in which we have the RIGHT and AUTHORITY to choose our own standards for living. Every generation of worshipers from the beginning of time has heard the voice of the enemy breathing this lie to make us like himself—failed usurpers of the kingdom of God!

This reality of my guilt in this area has recently become abundantly clear to me. Over the last few weeks, my wife and I have embarked on a complete lifestyle change in our eating habits. This may not seem to mean much to my readers, but as a couple whose hobbies are cooking and baking (we admit without shame that we are diehard *foodies*) this has been a challenging journey. As we began this Christian weight loss program, we began to further investigate the subject of nutrition, health, and the food industry. I will give you a warning: if you do not want to see some of your favorite foods suddenly become repulsive, then take my advice and do not follow my example. When we discovered what we were actually doing to our bodies by indulging in various foods, conviction come upon us. God began to speak to us about how we were seeing ourselves. I assumed that when it came to the area of food and nutrition that I was the one who had the authority to choose. The truth, however, is that we are *"not our own; you were bought with a price. Therefore honor God with your body"* (1 Corinthians 6:20). Paul, on more than one occasion, reminds us that *"We are the temple of the Holy Spirit"* (1 Corinthians 3:16, 6:19). This thought has given us a new avenue in our lives to glorify God as we strive to worship Him even in our eating.

You might be thinking that considering God in your diet is a somewhat radical idea. Actually, this is far beyond an issue about food. This is an issue of authority. Consider what Satan attempted to do in usurping God's authority. Isaiah 14:13-14 records a time when the enemy sought to challenge God. The following lists the five *I wills* of the passage and I have taken the liberty to explain the essence of those statements:

> <u>I *will* ascend to heaven</u>: I *will* establish my kingdom.
> <u>I *will* raise my throne</u>: I *will* establish my power.
> <u>I *will* sit enthroned</u>: I *will* establish my place of recognition.
> <u>I *will* ascend above the clouds:</u> I *will* establish my predominance.
> <u>I *will* make myself like the Most High:</u> I *will* establish my supremacy.

There is a progression in Satan's prideful thinking. It wasn't enough to only have a piece of heaven or a place of power. Satan wanted it all. He wanted to be God with all of the glory that is rightfully the Lord's. In a drastic and sudden way, Satan discovered that when it came to reigning supremely over all of creation there can only be One who will ever sit upon the throne!

Although his plan failed (as if he could have succeeded), Satan is now masterfully wreaking havoc upon God's people by leading them into the same damning progression which he plotted in heaven. After all, if the thought of having God's glory for himself was an attractive notion in a place void of any influence to solicit such a thought, how much more would we as lesser beings be attracted to the thought of becoming "like God?" (Genesis 3:5).

Satan is a brilliant foe. We underestimate his ability to infiltrate the church and destroy the purpose for which we exist as a church body—to worship the Lord. He does this in an ever-so-subtle way, and before we know it we have fully embraced the idea of usurping the authority of God in our lives. Consider the story of Hansel and Gretel as a framework for how Satan accomplished his plan. Did Hansel and Gretel one day decide to go to the witch's house and say, "Hey, I've got a great idea! Let's climb into someone's oven and let's get eaten for dinner!" They had no plans to be eaten by the witch, but they ended up there by first detouring from the path where they were supposed to be walking. Once away from where they needed to be, they were offered tasty delicacies which brought them further into the witch's lair. She, in turn, fattened them up to the point where they became helpless to her evil plot. There was a progression as to how they ended up in such a predicament.

In my own life, this story is a vivid reminder of Satan's cunningness to destroy our lives. Several years ago, in the midst of a thriving ministry, my life came to complete ruin. I never remember waking up and saying, "Today is the day in which I will decide to walk away from the Lord!" It was a subtle progression of believing that as a pastor I had to get the job done. Satan had suggested that "If I didn't do it, no one would." Buying in to this lie, I began to intensify my ministry by spending long hours focusing upon the needs of those I ministered to. Little did I realize, I was no longer leaving room for God to deal with those under my care. Instead, I felt I needed to be the savior of their pain and problems. I attempted to put myself in the place of God in seeing myself as the only one who was able to meet their needs. Like Lucifer who perched himself upon the pedestal of pride, I too, basked in my supremeness only to fall into the abyss of sin's stronghold.

We do not start off by saying, "Today, I think I will announce my supremacy to the world!" Instead, we begin by saying, "I am going to establish a little kingdom for myself. A place where I can make some decisions of my own and where I can establish my own set of standards." We convince ourselves that this kingdom of ours will pose no threat to God's kingdom. Like Eve in the Garden, we believe that the serpent's lie of making our own choice is perfectly fine with God. I have a little place of my own where I can be like God and make the choices of what is right and wrong.

What follows this mentality is the beginning of a downward spiral. A kingdom of one is never enough. It then becomes important that you establish a sense of power by attempting to control things which normally God would control. Adam and Eve were not satisfied with the fact that God willingly controlled all that went on in the Garden. They became attracted to the power He held. Even today, this attitude prevails in the church. Many individuals have adopted the position that it is their God given duty to submit an opinion about everything that goes on in the church. They determine that they must remain *in the know* and feel that their voice must be heard in all decisions made in the church body.

With the quest for power comes the need for recognition. Since it's your kingdom you're establishing, people have to recognize who you are. It must have been quite an ego boost for the couple in the Garden when the serpent had taken notice that they were being mistreated by the Lord. He gave them a sense of entitlement. They deserved not only to know but to be known. Certainly every creature in the Garden knew God, but this was their big chance to make a name for themselves. The serpent cunningly alluded to the fact that God may have been wrong. "Did God really say?" his voiced hissed.

"Perhaps we do know better," they thought, "Imagine what people will say of us if we let them in on knowledge that God did not reveal to others."

The result becomes clear. You are now the expert. You are bent on fulfilling the quest to "ascend above the clouds" and let everyone know that you have been given such glory and greatness. You are exempt from the boundaries set forth in God's Word as you have received new revelation which is privileged only for those whose eyes have been opened. Because God has not done a thorough enough job explaining His Word to others, you have been donned with the privilege of interpreting the meaning of what God really meant concerning His Word. This can be seen in today's *Latter Rain Movement, New Apostolic Reformation,* and *Extreme Prophetic Movements.* The teachers from these movements offer new revelation that supersedes Scriptural truth and espouse that they alone hold the keys to understanding the deeper truths concerning God. Be warned church!

The last step is a far leap from the initial step of simply desiring to have one corner of life in which you can call your own. The words "I will make myself like the Most High" is seldom ever spoken; however, it is lived out on a daily basis among countless numbers of people who have called themselves *Christians.* They live as if their lives are their own. They fashion God in the image they have created rather than the reality of who He is. They reserve the right of supremacy in choosing how, when, where and why they worship. They fashion their own truths, set their own boundaries and formulate their own beliefs concerning who God is to them. In essence, they create a supremacy in themselves which doesn't exist in God Himself—the ability to create a god that has never existed before.

Satan's strategy is devious but effective. He attempts to convince us that we are entitled to have a part of ourselves that is our very own. He alludes to the idea that God may be wrong about how He is to be served and worshiped. He woos us to believe that we are somehow a significant part of worship and gets us to buy in to the idea that God will share His glory with us. He then gives us a blueprint to fashion our own god from the use of our emotions, attitudes and desires that serve to produce a god which will fit comfortably under the rule of our kingdom.

Ultimately, the pinnacle goal of Satan's dirty little secret is in creating a god that you can rule. He wants God to worship you and change the place of position between Creator and creature. We may say to ourselves, "I could never do such a thing!" The reality, nonetheless, may be seen in our actions of daily life. Does God get the glory in every area of your life? Is He included in every decision in your life? Is God becoming more splendid and imposing in your life; or are you living life as you please and worship is something you do at church? The truth is, if God doesn't have the authority to influence every decision in your life, whether through His Word or prompting of His Spirit, then who is making those decisions? Worship is not something we do, it is who we are. We are always worshiping and bringing glory to something or someone in our lives. And while Satan will continue to spread his dirty little secret, we need to take an honest look at our lives and ask ourselves: "When it comes to worship, who are we really worshiping?"

Chapter Six

What We Must Fear

The fear of the Lord is the beginning of knowledge
Proverbs 1:7

. . . and he will delight in the fear of the Lord.
Isaiah 11:3

It's confession time. I am going out on a limb to be completely honest with you concerning a major flaw in my life: I am a *scaredy-cat*. Yes, all of my life I have battled a formidable foe called *fear*. As a child, it was instilled in me by my loving, but over-protective mother. Growing up, I learned that everything in life had the potential to be dangerous or harmful. Even now, she tells my children things like, "Don't touch anything" when they go to the bathroom or "Wash your hands" if they pet the dog. Although we laugh about her fear of germs, natural disasters and government conspiracies, her determination to keep me safe was not without consequence.

I cannot with good conscious blame all of my struggles in this area on my mother. It is one thing to be influenced as a child by what your parents exemplified in front of you, but it is another thing to develop your own ideas after you begin the process of maturity to adulthood. For instance, during my teenage years my friends and I were fans of watching the gory, *hack-n-slash* horror movies. In fact, in order to wear the "Horror Badge of Honor" in our youth group we would purposely look for movies that were more bloody, deranged and frightening. No one had to hold a gun to my head and say, "Watch this movie," nor did my parents threaten me with discipline if I refused to put the VHS tape in the player. This was a decision I made all on my own. I have now come to appreciate the words I heard several times from my youth pastor: "Garbage in, garbage out."

Sometimes the garbage out portion of that saying doesn't surface until years later. While I was pursing my undergraduate degree, I had the opportunity to make extra money (which is always an enticement for a poor college student) by occasionally working the third-shift security guard slot on weekends. It was an easy job and a break from my normal job of working on the night janitorial crew for the *General Council of the Assemblies of God National Offices*. The other major advantage was that I was able to study as much as I wanted in between my nightly rounds.

On one particular weekend, a New Year's Eve shift, I was informed that I would be the only one in the building complex due to the holiday. It wasn't so bad for the first and second hourly rounds, but as the night progressed my mind began to play tricks on me. I began to experience a very real sense of dread. To make matters worse, I had to walk through a dark underground tunnel that connected the power plant to the main complex. During the four o'clock shift, I remember scurrying down the dark tunnel thinking of every horror movie I had ever seen—*Alien, Predator, Silence of the Lambs*—you get the picture. Up ahead in the dark tunnel was a single door with a small window positioned at the top. Through it, I could see light and I knew that if I could just get to the door I would be safe. I frantically raced to the door as my mind had gotten the best of me. At last I reached it. I turned the knob, opened the door, screamed and almost fainted! To my surprise, on the other side of the door was a man holding a tool box. I'm sure I startled him as well; he thought he was the only person in the building. No one bothered to advise me that New Year's Day was the only day of the year that the records room could be shut down for maintenance.

This is a somewhat humorous story, but I believe that it served as a catalyst to what would follow in my life: years of suffering from panic attacks. When I hear the word *fear* I generally agree with the basic definition which means "a distressing emotion aroused by impending danger, evil, pain, etc . . . , whether the threat is real or imagined; the feeling or condition of being afraid." It doesn't take a genius to figure out that in this life there are healthy fears and unhealthy fears. For instance, a little child should be intensely afraid to run out into the street without first checking for traffic. Likewise, you should have some level of fear if you are in the middle of a golf course and bolts of lightning are zipping down all around you (to my shameful admission of movie viewing in my younger years, when I think of storms and golf courses, I think of *Caddyshack*). These are what we could coin as healthy fears.

Unhealthy fears, however, are not good. These are the fears which we have come to believe to be a real threat to our lives. In fact, the majority of psychologists have come to believe that we are born with only two natural fears: the fear of falling and the fear of loud noises. All other fears in life are learned. The healthy fears come about through the wisdom gleaned from experiencing life and the innate desire to preserve our lives. Unhealthy fears come about by our perceptions about life and how our minds have been conditioned to believe those perceptions. Just as I knew that aliens, predators and serial killers were not lurking in that dark tunnel in Springfield, Missouri, my mind still perceived the threat of their existence. Why? I had conditioned my mind to succumb to fearful thinking through watching countless hours of movies that promoted fear.

Over the last few years something strange has happened concerning society's view of fear. An entire generation has developed a somewhat twisted attitude towards it and has embraced the things which they should be fearful of as a means of entertainment and challenge. In a world of extreme sports, *Jackass* movies, viral submissions, and media blitzes, fear is no longer to be feared. Instead, it has become the ultimate thrill ride sought by many to enjoy the bragging rights to a few laughs and the spotlight of the internet. This frenzy of thrill-seeking has caused a desensitized perspective towards fear. Proof of this can be seen in watching a group of young people who think nothing of trying to surf a thirty-foot wave in dangerous riptides and yet at the same time have a genuine fear that global warming is going to destroy the world! The result is becoming clear—we are moving towards a world which no longer fears what we should and fears what we should not.

This attitude has, regrettably, invaded the church and caused the Body of Christ to casually approach worship like an extreme sport, looking for the ultimate thrill while not realizing the present danger it poses to their spiritual lives. The phrase "the fear of the Lord" is perhaps one of the most misunderstood concepts in Scripture. Because we have developed the idea that we are now living in the age of grace, we act as if the "fear of the Lord" is an Old Testament concept losing its modern day relevance. We've developed beliefs, via men such as Rob Bell, that God is a big softy who will overlook all of humanity's sins on the basis that His love would never punish His creation with the fires of Hell; after all, *Love Wins* right?

I will let you in on a little secret. God hasn't become soft in His old age (not that He ever ages); it's poor theology to think that He was a God of fire and judgment in the Old Testament who suddenly changed into a God of grace and mercy in the New Testament. Yet I believe many within the church see God in this manner. We see Jesus as the One who has pacified God's judgment, rather than the One who reconciled us to God. The sacrifice of Christ was not an appeasement for an angry God bent on destroying His creation. The sacrifice of Christ was necessary in order to bridge an uncrossable chasm between God and man. God was driven by His love, yet His love doesn't erase the reality of how He still views sin. Sin still leads to death, it still destroys lives, and it still holds devastating consequences for those who would indulge in its delicacies. For some reason, we've come to believe that God's love allows us to toy with the contagion of sin and remain immune from the judgment of a holy God.

This prevailing attitude is resulting in the loss of one of the most essential requirements for worship—the fear of the Lord. Proverbs 1:7 states, *"The fear of the Lord is the beginning of KNOWLEDGE [emphasis added]."* When we consider the implications of this verse, is it any wonder why it appears the church suffers from an anemic faith? Because we have skirted the subject of the "fear of the Lord" in the practice of worship and have opted for the more comfortable aspects of God—His love, grace, mercy and friendship—we've become content to know *of* God rather than actually knowing God.

To better understand how this affects our worship, we need to examine the idea of what it means to *fear God*. First of all, there is a part of us that should be *afraid* of God. As I mentioned before, when people came into the presence of a holy and awesome God they were overcome with fear. He is the Creator of the Universe; He holds the keys to life and death; and He is eternally worthy of all glory, honor and praise! Can you imagine standing before the Almighty? It's not like sitting in the pew of a Catholic church looking up at a wimpy, weak and famished Jesus on a cross, feeling sorry for the poor guy. No, the God that we will one day stand before is a terrifying, all-consuming fire who is able to, with a single breath from His mouth, annihilate all of His creation if He so chooses.

Beyond the thought that the "fear of the Lord" means to be afraid of God, to fear Him also means to give Him our reverence, honor and awe that is due Him. True worship cannot be approached in any other way. Imagine yourself on an airplane about to land in the midst of an extremely dense fog. The pilot cannot visually see the runway but with the aid of the plane's navigational instruments and some dim lighting on the runway, a successful landing is possible. As the plane makes its descent, the pilot decides to do something completely foolish. Rather than respecting the readings of the plane's navigational system and the lights tracing the runway, he decides to land the plane trusting only on the things that have made him feel good about being a pilot. I don't know about you, but I would not want to be on that plane!

The pilot should have, at some point, been awed by the complex navigational system of the plane. The realization that he was at the mercy of the plane's ability to fly and his desperate need for the runway lights to provide a pathway to a safe landing, should have resulted in a respect for the technological advances that surrounded him. By ignoring these things, he forfeited the adequate knowledge available to him to land successfully. Author and speaker John Bevere points out this thought concerning the fear of the Lord:

> Our love of God is limited to our lack of holy fear . . . You can only love someone to the extent that you know them. If your image of God falls short of who He is, then you have but a surface knowledge of the One you love. True love is founded in the truth of who God really is. Do you think He reveals His heart to those who take Him lightly?[14]

He goes on to cite Psalm 25:14 which states:

> *The secret of the Lord is with those who fear Him,*
> *and He will show them His covenant.*

We cannot come to a deeper place of knowing God if we first do not establish our reverence and awe toward the Person of God.

Sadly, there is an ever-increasing casualness in our approach to worship. We strive to make people feel relaxed and at ease so they can enjoy the service. We promote the *come as you are* premise and invite the presence of the Living and Holy God in our midst without considering the question: "Are we ready to approach His throne?" You may be thinking, "Yes, I am based on the fact that I'm a Christian and because of the blood of Jesus that allows me to have '*confidence to enter the Most Holy Place*'" (Hebrews 10:19). The problem with simply accepting one's position based solely on that claim is that Hebrews further explains a reason to not be so confident in approaching God's throne:

> *If we deliberately keep on sinning after we have received knowledge of the truth, no sacrifice for sins is left, but only a fearful expectation of judgment and raging fire that will consume the enemies of God. Anyone who rejected the Law of Moses died*

without mercy on the testimony of two or three witnesses. How much more severely do you think a man deserves to be punished who has trampled the Son of God under foot, who has treated as an unholy thing the blood of the covenant that has sanctified him and who has insulted the Spirit of grace? For we know him who said, 'It is mine to avenge; I will repay,' and again, 'The Lord will judge His people.' It is a dreadful thing to fall into the hands of a living God (Hebrews 10:26-32)

On one hand, the author of Hebrews gives us a great sense of belonging in the throne room of God because of the shed blood of Christ. On the other hand, he clearly reminds us that if we do not show the proper reverence for God by actually considering what Jesus' sacrifice fulfilled in our lives—the removing of and the ability not to sin, then "no sacrifice for sins is left." Did you catch that? The very thing that has granted us access into the throne room of God can also be taken away. The sacrifice of Christ is a blessing for those who accept the reality of its purpose and a curse for those who choose to profane it by sinful living.

The lack of the fear of the Lord has cultivated a permissive attitude toward sin and worldliness within the church. We have come to believe in the "Don't judge me!" mentality when it comes to our sin. We act as if God's grace and love looks beyond our deliberate and contradictory lifestyles that profane the Holy Spirit which dwells in us. And then we have the audacity to proclaim that "We know God!"

I believe that the *proof is in the pudding* when it comes to gauging whether or not we are a people who have come to fear the Lord. When you think about all that consumes the life of the American believer, you can get an idea of how far we have strayed from truly appropriating the fear of the Lord in our lives. Compare the average activities that culture seeks to indulge for pleasure and you will discover that there is essentially no difference between the world and the church. We watch the same movies, visit the same beaches, attend various sporting venues, watch the same television shows, shop at the same stores, and frequent the same restaurants. Not that all of these are necessarily bad on every level, but my point remains that when it comes to finding pleasure in life, we seek after the same things. Unfortunately, the modern day picture of Christianity suggests otherwise.

If we are honest with ourselves, I believe that we would be in agreement that when it comes to the way we live our lives, seldom do we base our decisions upon the fear of the Lord. We typically view our faith through the lens of what we *cannot do* verses the lens of what we *can do* in pleasing God. In areas of question, we do not consider what Scripture says on the matter. Instead, we opt for the modern day church's culturally acceptable standard that aims to live as close to the line without crossing it. Sure, we want to be holy but not to the point where it takes away all of the freedoms we have in enjoying the pleasures of life. A.W. Tozer makes a powerful point explaining his concern for the lack of genuineness in the Christian faith:

> There should be the terror of seeing ourselves in violent contrast to the holy, holy, holy God. Unless we come into this place of conviction and pain, I am not sure how deep and real our repentance will ever be.[15]

He goes on to suggest that our lacking to fear God is not a question of our uncleanliness but it is a question of our *awareness.* Like the world, we have become unclean and appear to be "almost totally unaware of it."[16]

Could this be true? Could we be so unclean and unaware that we have lost sight of the fear of God? Let's consider some pointed questions:

- Do you sit and watch movies or television programs that promote sex, violence, adultery, homosexuality and profane language without even considering if what you are viewing is offensive to God?

- Are you more scheduled in following your favorite sports team, Facebook, Twitter and email than you are in following the Lord in the Word and prayer?

- Have you actually prayed about things that are questionable to your witness (the use of alcohol, tobacco, secular music, books and magazines) to see if they are in any way affecting your walk of faith?

- Are you defensive or offended when someone points out an area of your life that is out of line with Scripture and quickly use the "Don't judge me card" to validate your actions or activities?

Those are difficult questions, but how we answer them will speak volumes about how unclean or unaware we may actually be.

The life that delights in the fear of the Lord is a life which results in holiness. Nancy DeMoss describes one of my favorite definitions of holiness by explaining "to be holy is to be wholly satisfied with Christ."[17] Living life in such a way that aims to totally satisfy Christ with your life and to be totally satisfied with Christ in all of your life is the true evidence of a person that fears the Lord. If our relationship with the Lord is not sufficient enough to make us stand in awe of who He is at all times and causes us to turn to other things that are not spiritually beneficial, we must face the truth that our delight is not in Christ. In reality, the actions of our lives speak of our delights. We may say we delight in Jesus, but if we live otherwise and search to be satisfied through other things, we have lost the fear of the Lord.

Isaiah 11 is one of the great prophetic chapters of the Old Testament that points to the coming of the promised Messiah. One of the qualities which set this Promised One apart was God's Spirit and character resting upon Him. Not only would He exemplify God's wisdom, understanding, counsel, knowledge and power, but He would also delight in the fear of the Lord. This may sound strange as we usually think of delighting in something as being associated with pleasure and satisfaction. The English word *delight* means "a high degree of pleasure or satisfaction, something that gives great pleasure." The Hebrew concept of delight expands our modern day idea of pleasure and satisfaction by literally associating it with the idea of "aroma and sweet smell." In one sense, the promised Messiah is one who would take pleasure in breathing in the sweet aroma that comes from a life of fearing the Lord. Our modern terminology might suggest that the fear of the Lord brings about a fresh breath of air.

Because the worship relationship brings us to a greater place of intimacy with Christ, we in turn should also become more and more like Jesus in our lives. If He delighted in the fear of the Lord and saw it as a breath of fresh air during His life on earth then shouldn't we as well? Our continual drive to find pleasure in this life speaks to the simple truth that we are no longer a people who truly stand in awe of God. If we were captured by the majesty, splendor and wonder of our Lord, then nothing in this world would compete with our attention and affection for Him. If we are to return to a place of worshiping the Lord *in spirit and in truth* then we must have the fear of the Lord. As Paul said in 2 Corinthians 6:17-18:

> 'Therefore come out from among them and be separate' says the Lord 'and do not touch what is unclean and I will welcome you. Touch no unclean thing and I will receive you. I will be a Father to you and you will be my sons and my daughters, says the Lord Almighty.

If we are to ever return to a place where, like Christ, we delight in the fear of the Lord, then we must appropriate this verse for our lives. What we must fear is the lack of fearing God. Only when we see holiness as the means of delighting in the Lord, will true worship be restored to the church. No longer can we be satisfied with a nominal Christianity that sees holy living as the exception rather than the rule. We must begin to validate our claims of worshiping an Almighty, Holy God through the actions of holiness that permeates our everyday lives. His ways, His plans and His desires should consume our passions and cause us to live fully satisfied in being His and His alone. If God is truly worthy of our worship, then fearing Him should be nothing less than a fresh breath of air in the midst of a stagnant and putrid world reeking with the stench of lesser things.

Chapter Seven

Who is Really Being Offended?

And do not grieve the Holy Spirit of God, with whom you were sealed for the day of redemption.
Ephesians 4:30

Do not put out the Spirit's fire.
1 Thessalonians 5:19

The world I now live in is drastically different than in the days of my youth. I remember a time when a right given to us in our constitution known as the *Freedom of Speech* allowed Americans to voice their opinions in the public arena of religion and politics without legal interference from the authorities. No matter how right, wrong, bigoted or offensive they were, people were entitled to their opinions. As a believer in Christ, I've appreciated my Constitutional right to freely speak my mind concerning my beliefs. Unfortunately, I have come to discover that the country I live in reeks of hypocrisy. The freedom allotted to us in the First Amendment is being challenged on several fronts. Americans have now become overly sensitive, and we've adopted the idea of political correctness as a way to avoid people getting their feelings hurt—even if it is over the truth.

As if that was not enough, the failure to be politically correct can spawn public outrage calling for justice to be served on an offender. Voiced opinions, which contradict the beliefs of another, can potentially lead to civil action or even worse a hate crime. We hear stories of people being prosecuted for doing something as innocent as offering ham sandwiches to students when a Muslim child is present. We dare not say anything on television or radio that would negatively allude in the slightest way to a person's gender, race, religion or sexual orientation. Even if we "didn't mean it that way," we can now be found guilty for whatever comes from our mouths. The foolishness in all of this is that it is not the context that determines the nature of the speech but the interpreter's belief of what the speaker actually meant. Thus, the entire premise of hate speech is defined subjectively by the hearer creating a self-made standard of meaning.

As a result of this madness, society is emphasizing the need to become more sensitive to the beliefs of others. The idea of *sensitivity training* has now surfaced as a way to ensure that leaders and those in the public's eye can do their jobs effectively without being an offense to anyone. The word *sensitive* carries the idea that one is aware of and responsive to the needs or feelings of others; however, in our new perceived understanding, being sensitive includes the removal of anything from our words, actions and attitudes that might bring about an offense to others. Because offense in our culture equates the idea that it is wrong to hurt someone's feelings, we have created a culture which has become increasingly ultra-sensitive to anything that may remotely offend someone who views life differently than we do.

This unfortunate shift in cultural practice has also permeated the culture of the church. Beyond the idea of promoting a seeker-sensitive church environment, the infiltration of the ultra-sensitive attitude aims to go much farther in attempting to become all things to all people in the worship setting. Welcome to the Emergent church! Its rise in America has encapsulated the idea of ultra-sensitivity within the four walls of the church to the point where if you do not like all of the truths that are written in Scripture, you can choose to develop your own non-offensive understanding of God's Word. The Emergent church is a growing movement. Its draw is in finding one's own path to God; a path filled with goodness, happiness and things that work best for you. It's free from the burden of being offended by things like the cross, sin and hell. It is the perfect place for finding yourself and discovering a God that fits perfectly to your way of life. In essence, it is a man-focused, man-serving and man-sensitive attempt to worship God.

In arguing the perspective of Emergent theology, one could defend its existence by promoting the idea that by creating a non-offensive environment that is focused upon the needs of man, the church is better positioned to build relationships to win people for Christ. One could further that argument by submitting that biblical teaching is not as important as developing your own understanding as to whom God is and then worshiping Him through that understanding. In doing so, a person does not have to be offended by being told what God demands, commands or requires of a worshipper. People should not be made to feel guilty, ashamed, convicted or unworthy; after all, God is full of love, grace and mercy. Because Jesus rebuked those who subscribed to religion, the Emergent church is concerned with the relationship of the heart; to them, following one's heart is the only way in a postmodern society to establish truth.

Although most Evangelical churches would not be in agreement with Emergent theology, practically speaking, they have adopted some of its ideology. It seems that many churches are striving to become more appealing to their community. There is great concern over how visitors may view a church's worship experience; consequently, this has resulted in adapting the worship service to meet the expectations of a secular mindset. The problem, however, is a church cannot aim to be pleasers of man and pleasers of God at the same time. True worship cannot center upon being sensitive to man's feelings and man's perspective without first considering the heart of God on the matter (1 Thessalonians 2:4-6). Contrary to popular belief, the purpose of the church is not to win people for Christ. The purpose of the church is to worship the Lord! Evangelism will certainly flow from true worship, but glorifying God is the reason the church exists. This increased sensitivity to meeting the needs of men has impeded the impact of what worship should produce within the life of the church.

If we are to ever experience the life of worship available to us in Christ, then the church needs to implement a sensitivity training of its own. Have we ever considered our hypocrisy in taking measures to ensure that we are not offending our fellow man while not considering if we are offending the Spirit of God in the process? Think about it. We attempt to make church an inoffensive place where imperfect and unyielded people are led to believe that God is accepting of the condition of their lives. Sadly, in doing so, we offend the Holy Spirit by ignoring Him and treating His conviction as an ungodly activity.

In almost every church staff meeting, we discuss elements of the worship service and contemplate if people are going to be comfortable with what we feel God wants to do. How often do we contemplate if we're doing anything that may be offensive to God? How much do we consider the actions that demean His presence in our church? Think about how offensive it is for God to sit in our churches at times. We plan entire services with the goal of hoping that people will enjoy it and squelch the freedom of giving God center stage to do as He pleases among His people. I can almost hear Him saying, "Hey, the reason you have church is for Me, and yet you're doing your best to ignore My presence here!"

In both the corporate setting and the individual life, we need to cultivate a greater sensitivity to the Spirit of the Lord. Ephesians 4:30 tells us:

> *And do not grieve the Holy Spirit, with whom you*
> *were sealed for the day of redemption.*

Paul's command is for us not to offend the Spirit of God who has authenticated His work and presence in our lives. Whether or not we are aware of this fact, our lives are a representation of the Lord. Isn't it interesting when an athlete does something so offensive such as illegal dog fighting, sexually assaulting a woman in the back room of a nightclub, or killing a pedestrian while driving drunk, that we become outraged and wholeheartedly support the given consequences of their actions through both the legal and organizational system. We would be foolish to think otherwise. Yet in our arrogance we hold God to a much lower standard. Seldom is our prayer, "God give us what we deserve."

God is a God of mercy; but we must remember that does not excuse our actions in offending Him. At times, I think that we believe that God has extra thick skin and what may offend the average person would not come close to bothering God. In reality, the opposite is true. As humans, we are hardened to sin's deceitfulness; we can, in essence, participate in a sinful act and think nothing of it. But with God, He is holy and He cannot and will not tolerate sin of any measure no matter how insignificant it may seem to us. This is proof that we have become desensitized to the work of the Holy Spirit in our lives. Tozer supports this notion in describing one of the essential works the Spirit perfects in our lives:

> One of the very greatest calamities which sin has brought upon us is the debasement of our emotions. We laugh at things which are not funny; we find pleasure in acts which are beneath our human dignity; and we rejoice in objects which should have no place in our affections . . . The world's artificial pleasures are all but evidence that the human race has to a large extent lost its power to enjoy true pleasures of life and has been forced to substitute for them false and degrading thrills. The work of the Holy Spirit is, among other things, to rescue redeemed man's emotions, to restring his harp and open again the wells of sacred joy which have been stopped by sin.[18]

Has the Holy Spirit been allowed to do the work necessary in our lives? Do we allow our emotions and desires to be guided by our impulses or do we consult the Spirit of the Lord before responding to them? Some of us are so careful in our social circles as not to be offensive in any way towards those we mingle with. We even teach our kids in public settings to be polite and to watch what they say in order to not embarrass their parents or offend others. We simply do not want to be offensive in any way, shape or form. My point is clear: we stop short of nothing in order to avoid offending others, and yet we fail to exercise the same consideration for the Holy Spirit in our lives.

Consider this analogy. Every year, we have what has become known as the "Birthday Bash". Because we have four birthdays for our four youngest children, who are all no more than four years apart, and whose birthdays all take place between mid-May and mid-August, we found it much easier to have one giant party. We want to bless our little ones and provide them with a joyous time of celebration. I could not imagine if my wife and I went through the pain-staking measures to provide this joyous party and paid an expensive price in making it happen, only to discover my children would rather go play in the city's garbage dump. As parents, we would be saddened over the fact that they would want to choose something other than what we had worked so hard to make special for them. We would consider our children ungrateful at best, wicked at heart. Yet how often do we treat the Spirit of Christ in this manner? He has provided us with the celebration of abundant life, paid an incredible price to make it available, and has ensured a time of incredible joy and pleasure; yet we choose to play in the garbage pit of the world.

As much as I struggle with the over-emphasis on pleasing man in our church services, the root of the problem lies in pleasing ourselves; however, I believe this is partially due to the lack of understanding as to what worship means. Worship goes far beyond the Sunday morning activities of what takes place in a church service. I'm not a fan of calling the portion of the service where the church sings songs of praise and worship as being *worship*. In actuality, this is only a small expression of worship. Instead, worship is how we live our lives before the Lord. It is a constant attempt of making our lives a holy and pleasing response of love to the Lord. In essence, worship encompasses the whole of life. Because we fail to see this dynamic, we tend to compartmentalize our lives into areas of sacred and secular.

Paul makes an interesting statement in 1 Thessalonians 5:19 that states, *"Do not put out the Spirit's fire."* In examining this passage, we need to ask ourselves two questions: "What exactly is the *Spirit's fire?"* and "How is it possible to extinguish it?" When I think of the Spirit's "fire" I am reminded of a command given to Aaron and his sons concerning the fire on the altar of sacrifice. Leviticus 6:8-13 contains a series of commands reminding the priests that the fire *"must be kept burning on the altar continuously; it must not go out"* (v.13). Three times within these verses, Aaron was commanded to keep the fire burning at all costs. It is not difficult to see the parallels to this Old Testament command and Paul's command of not quenching the Spirit's fire in our lives. The altar now remains in our hearts and the sacrifice to be placed upon that altar is our lives (Romans 12:1-2).

Although Aaron and his sons received these instructions, we find a few chapters later in Leviticus the awful price that Aaron's sons paid for not taking the sanctity of God's fire seriously. In short, Nadab and Abihu chose to play around with God's fire and paid for it with their lives! They "offered unauthorized fire before the Lord, contrary to his command" (Leviticus 10:1). And how did God take this act of disobedience?

So fire came out from the presence of the Lord and consumed them, and they died before the Lord (Leviticus 10:2).

I would venture to say that if Nadab and Abihu would have been more sensitive to the Spirit of the Lord, they may have enjoyed long and prosperous lives in serving the Lord.

As good grace-based Christians, we want to dismiss this story as being one of God's extreme judgments of His Old Testament days. The issue with this sort of thinking is that the New Testament is laced with warnings against treating the Spirit of God with the same measure of contempt as shown by Nadab and Abihu. If it wasn't possible to extinguish the Spirit's fire in our lives, then why are we warned not to? In Romans 8, Paul makes something crystal clear: if we are not being fueled by the Spirit's fire, then we will die! (Romans 8:5-14).

The lesson to be learned in the story of Nadab and Abihu is that they were struck down during an *act of worship.* The *strange fire* was offered unto the Lord, and yet it was far from being an acceptable sacrifice. This begs the questions, "Does God accept whatever worship we offer Him? Is He pleased with whatever token of praise and appreciation we see fit to give Him, or does He require something more?" The one thing I cannot express enough is that worship is not dependent upon what we make of it—it is dependent upon what God requires. The Spirit of God is more sensitive than we believe Him to be. He doesn't have to accept the leftovers of half-hearted worship founded from nominal Christian living based on the fact that Jesus died for our sins. Our God is a *Consuming Fire*, and just as parents warn their children, fire is something that is not to be played with!

Paul lays out a full-proof plan to keep the Spirit's fire in our lives from being extinguished. One of the most important things which we must keep at the forefront of our lives is to *"not treat prophecies with contempt"* (1 Thessalonians 5:20). The word *prophecies*, or literally *prophetic utterances*, goes beyond the common idea of being words that are predictive. The more applicable meaning of the word is "a discourse emanating from divine inspiration and declaring the purposes of God."[19] It is what God is commanding us, and more specifically, it is what God is speaking to us now through His Word. Paul's words could be paraphrased to mean, "Do not despise, ignore, or disobey the Word of God which He has spoken to you." Treating prophecies with contempt is not a matter of despising or ignoring a *word* that someone believes God has for us, but it is a blatant rejection of Scripture—God's Word to us! Whether it is the Emergent church holding to the belief that Scripture is not God's absolute truth or a local congregation basing its worship practices upon what seems relevant to culture, we are playing with fire when we fail to heed God's Word.

We cannot pretend to go through the ritual of worship when our lives are in direct disobedience to the Word of the Lord. This is why God told the church in Laodicea that their lukewarm, middle of the road, and compromising lifestyle of worshiping Him literally makes Him sick (Revelation 3:16). If we are not conscious of the relationship between God's Word and our lives, we cannot begin worshiping the Lord in *truth*. Ignoring the Spirit's voice of truth while attempting to offer worship to the Lord is the flint that sparks the flame of strange fire.

Another way we can avoid quenching the Spirit's fire is to develop the practice of *testing everything* (1 Thessalonians 5:21). Too often we participate in activities that appear to be centered on worship. Our mentality has produced the belief that if something sounds, looks or presents itself like Christianity, then it must be worthy of our attention and participation. Keep in mind that Nadab and Abihu appeared to be making the appropriate sacrifices to the Lord. To the naked eye, it would have been impossible to distinguish between the fire that burned on the altar of the Lord and the fire that Aaron's sons offered. Let's face it, fire looks like fire no matter where it is burning; conversely, we must realize the vast difference between the fire and its source.

We are not entirely clear as to what this violation in Leviticus detailed, but many commentators agree it had to do with Aaron's sons offering incense at an inappropriate time and using a fire that did not originate from the altar of the Lord. Symbolically, incense equates the idea of worship before the throne of the Lord. In essence, Nadab and Abihu offered *unauthorized worship* unto the Lord. The source of the fire, which is also indicative of the Holy Spirit, was not of God. This is why Paul stresses to "test everything." When it comes to worship, God does not excuse our ignorance in offending Him. Because we have the Spirit of the Living God within us, we have an obligation not to fall into deception. We deceive ourselves when we fail to test the things which affect our worship of the Lord. To gravitate towards teachings, movements and activities without first testing it in light of God's Word is nothing short of foolishness. We may be wowed by the supernatural and the fire that is blazing around us, and it may even seem like the incense of worship before the Lord; however, to make a decision based on your excitement and enthusiasm over what is happening versus seeking the Lord in the matter may prove to be a very costly decision for your life.

Jesus warned of a great deception that would take place in the last days (Matthew 24:4-28). Although I cannot extensively discuss this deception in the context of this book, I am concerned with the emphasis upon angelic visitations; bizarre manifestations of the supernatural; and teachings that promote *deeper revelation* given to self-proclaimed New Apostles, arising in today's church. Many are flocking for a powerful experience where signs and wonders abound; yet how sure are we in knowing that what is transpiring is not an offering of *strange fire* before the Lord? When experience cannot be substantiated through the truth of God's Word, we find ourselves in a very dangerous place; and in the same vein as Emergent theology, a worship built upon appealing to the senses of man is carelessly playing with fire.

Paul concludes his prescription to keep the Spirit's fire burning in our lives by holding *"on to the good"* and avoiding *"every kind of evil"* (1 Thessalonians 21-22). Typically, we attribute *holding* something as grasping with the option of eventually letting it go. Paul's usage denotes an idea of checking the steering of a ship in order to ensure that it is going the right direction. Paul intends for us to realize that the life we have in the Spirit is to be firmly grasped, secured and kept from changing direction. Unlike Nadab and Abihu, who for a brief moment in their life released their grasp upon what they knew to be the "good" commands of the Lord, we cannot chose to steer our lives in whatever direction we desire to go. Both Proverbs 14:12 and 16:25 tells us:

> There is a way that seems right to a man, but in the
> end it leads to death.

At all costs, we must not let go of the truth we have been given concerning how we are to live our lives as the children of God!

The second half to Paul's command is to "avoid every kind of evil." This statement is in complete contrast to the idea of grasping the good. This is a deliberate action of pushing away something that is coming towards us. The "every kind" of evil goes beyond evil or sinful actions to encompass even the idea of the appearance of evil. The Septuagint would suggest that "every kind of evil" includes "that which strikes the eye or is exposed to view." The Spirit's fire within us can be compromised by participating in activities which would remotely suggest that we are not adhering to the standards of God's Word. Although Nadab and Abihu were dressed up in priestly garments representing "worshipers of the Lord," they had filled their censors with incense and fire that violated God's commands. We too cannot expect to believe that just because we have been dressed up in the priestly garments of Christianity we are free to fill the censors of our hearts with incense and fire that the Lord will not accept. Each time we compromise our witness by indulging in things that cannot possibly bring glory to God we will no doubt grieve the Spirit of God within us and put out the Spirit's fire.

If we truly desire that our lives be a *"living sacrifice that is holy and pleasing to God"* (Romans 12:1), then we must take the appropriate measures to become sensitive to the presence of the Holy Spirit in our lives. We must purposely consider what the Lord thinks about our actions, attitudes, motives, words, activities and beliefs. He has given us His standard of how He is to be worshiped. Creating the *come as you are* approach to worship so prevalent in the church today is placing strange fire in the censors of today's worshipers. The only course of action that will steer the vessel of genuine worship into safe harbors is in keeping the Spirit's fire ablaze in our hearts—and that may actually offend certain people whose sole desire is to be happy, comfortable and complacent while in the presence of a holy God!

Chapter Eight

The Secret Lives
of Worshipers

*But when you pray, go into your room, and close
your door and pray to your Father who is unseen.
Then your Father who sees what is done in secret,
will reward you.*
Matthew 6:6

*Take me away with you—let us hurry! Let the king
bring me into his chambers*
Song of Solomon 1:4

A few years ago while leading worship, I spontaneously broke out with a song in a moment of Spirit-led inspiration that has now become one of the most intimate and powerful break-through songs of my worship ministry. This song often connects with those who desperately desire to be in the presence of the Lord. What is even more surprising is the simplicity of the lyrics:

*Take me away to the secret place.
Where it's only You.
Come away, come away, come away with me.*

The intense hunger evident in the Body of Christ is due to our feeding upon food which does not satisfy the hunger and thirst of our souls. We have lost sight of what it truly means to be worshipers and we've attempted to fill the void with lesser things in the hope of experiencing a morsel of glory from heaven. We read stories of the great men and women of God that serve as models of inspiration to our Christian heritage and see their lives as being the exception rather than the rule. It is as if these saints of old had been given a special blessing from heaven that allowed them a greater privilege of access into the Holy of Holies of God.

Working through my graduate studies, I've been given the opportunity to examine the lives of these great men and women of God—Evan Roberts, Charles Finney, Catherine Booth, Jonathan Edwards, Fanny Crosby, John Wesley, Duncan Campbell, Amy Carmichael, David Brainerd, Andrew Murray and many others who, by their own right, were ones who had touched the heart of God as *worshipers.* It wasn't what they taught, wrote or even contributed to the heritage of the Christian faith that made these saints of old stand out throughout the course of time; rather, it was how they worshiped the Lord. In studying them, I have come to discover two very important observations. First, these inspiring individuals were no different than us in being men and women who have come into relationship with Jesus Christ. Secondly, they all had to *do something* in order to become the people they became in Christ.

For too long the church has fed itself on a diet of bad theology. In today's church, the moment that we suggest that a Christian must do something in order to receive something from the Lord the cry is legalism. After all, our salvation is free right? Grace has become the proudly worn badge for apathetic and nominal Christian living. We do not have to do anything at all to have salvation, so let's live that way. In the wake of embracing this belief about salvation, a famine has taken place. The undernourished understanding of what it actually means to be saved has caused countless numbers of believers to miss out on the greater life that could be potentially given to them in Christ. Salvation is not given to us as a pass to go to heaven.

It is the giving of a new life in the kingdom of God. It is not a one-time event, but rather it is a continuous, organic process which changes a soul from a perpetual existence of death and decay to one of eternal life. The eternal life we have been given doesn't begin in heaven—it starts now!

This diet of poor theology has created a generation of spiritual obese saints whose lives are saturated with toxic spiritual food. They sit lazily on their comfy recliners of life exerting no spiritual exercise and doing absolutely nothing but waiting for the day when they use their free pass to eat at the *eternal life buffet* waiting for them in heaven. I'm still trying to find the scripture that tells me, "Now that you've received Jesus as your Savior you're all set, and you have absolutely nothing to do but wait to receive your heavenly mansion."

Consider these verses of scripture that speak against the common ideology of salvation:

> "... *continue to work out your salvation with fear and trembling*" (Philippians 2:12)

> "*For if the message spoken by angels was binding, and every act of disobedience received is just punishment, how shall we escape if we ignore such a great salvation?*" (Hebrews 2:3)

> "*What good is it, my brothers, if a man claims to have faith but has no deeds? Can such a faith save him?*" (James 2:14)

> "*Like new born babies, crave pure spiritual milk, so that by it you may grow up in your salvation, now that you have tasted that the Lord is good*" (1 Peter 2:2)

These verses, along with others, suggest that God is not the only One who works in the *process* of salvation. I will admit there is absolutely nothing we can do that will grant us salvation. We cannot obtain salvation by any of our own merits. This is clearly a gift of God (Ephesians 2:8-9). However, receiving the gift and opening the gift are two entirely different things. God doesn't give us the gift of salvation so that we can keep it on the shelf of our lives and do absolutely nothing with it. When He gives us this gift He demands that we do something with it. This very thought is what separates those who will make their mark in history as being exemplary pictures of true worshipers and those who will idly pass through this life like a vapor in the wind.

When we come to Christ, we have been given everything we need for life and godliness (2 Peter 1:3). The problem is that too many proclaiming Christians only have a *theological knowledge* of their salvation rather than a *living knowledge* in being saved. Sure, we can say things like, "God loves us and we are to love others." How true that is. After all, the greatest commandment is to love God and to love others. But how often do we actually experience loving God and telling others what loving God truly means. Jesus, in the Gospel of John, told His disciples, *"If anyone loves me, he will obey my commands"* (14:23); and with no mincing of words He also told them, *"If you obey my commands, you will remain in my love"* (15:10). God's attempt to bring us into proper relationship with Him has everything to do with His commitment to love us unconditionally. Those who understand this dynamic also understand that His pleasure, favor and grace upon our lives only fits into the context of our obedience towards Him. The person who has a living knowledge in their salvation understands that the wonderful blessings which accompany the Christian life are only bestowed upon those who earnestly live in such a manner that pleases God. Otherwise, Jesus' emphatic statements such as the following are nothing more than hyperbole and scare tactics:

> *"If anyone does not remain in me [speaking of obedience and bearing fruit] he is like a branch that is thrown away and withers"* (John 15:6)

> *"Not everyone who says to me 'Lord, Lord,' will enter the kingdom of heaven, but only he who DOES [emphasis added] the will of my Father who is in heaven"* (Matthew 7:21)

*"If anyone would come after me, he must DENY
[emphasis added] himself, TAKE UP [emphasis
added] his cross, and FOLLOW [emphasis added]
me. For whoever wants to save his life will lose it,
but whoever LOSES [emphasis added] his life for
me will find it"* (Matthew 16:24,25)

The question that we must ask ourselves in order to begin
to move away from only having a theological knowledge and
gravitating towards actually living our salvation is, "What must I
do to obtain such a life as those who have gone before and have
lived beyond the cultural norm of the expected Christian life?" All
of these men and women which we have come to see as spiritual
giants had a secret life which was discovered after their passing
into their heavenly reward.

Before we can have the kind of secret life which brings a living
knowledge of our salvation, we must first begin to understand
the necessity for the secret life and how it relates to worshiping
the Father in spirit and in truth. In his book, *With Christ in the
School of Prayer,* Andrew Murray explains the reasoning behind
our need to find this secret place:

> God is a God who hides Himself to the carnal eye.
> As long as in our worship of God we are chiefly
> occupied with our own thoughts and exercises,
> we will not meet Him Who is a Spirit, the Unseen
> One. But to the man who withdraws himself from
> all that is of the world and man and waits for God
> alone, the Father will reveal Himself . . . The secrecy
> of the inner chamber and the closed door, the
> entire separation from everything around us, is an
> image of the inner sanctuary, the secret of God's
> tabernacle. It is there within the veil that our spirit
> truly comes in contact with the Invisible One.[20]

Unless we have that secret place, that world God creates only for
His child to freely roam in the fields existing within the Father's
heart, we cannot possibly know more about our salvation than

what is written on the pages of a book. The Bible will fall short of being the living Word of God and will have as much appeal to our lives as a common textbook.

There is something intimate that transpires in the secret place where God and man come together to commune as one. Without this time of developing a secret life, the life of worship cannot be born in the heart of the believer. Inherent to the idea of worship is *intimacy*. Just as the sexual union of a married couple creates a greater sense of oneness between the husband and wife, the secret intimate life of the believer with his Lord solidifies the process of becoming one with the Father. It is in the secret place where the layers of the heart are stripped away. We allow ourselves to come before the Lord with a naked vulnerability as we become conscious of offering our exposed heart to the Lover of our Soul for the sake of bringing Him pleasure. And like the couple who by their act of intimacy creates life, the intimacy we have with the Lord begins the process by which God births in us the living experience of salvation.

Genesis 4:1 paints an interesting picture when we consider this type of intimacy that the Lord desires with us. The Hebrew word *yada,* which takes on several meanings, carries a foundational meaning of *knowing.* Adam "knew Eve and they conceived" refers to the act of sexual intercourse; however, the deeper intention of this word communicates the idea that beyond the bounds of carnal knowledge there is an intimacy based upon dedicating one's love, trust and affection to another. The result of knowing someone in this manner creates *life* within the relationship.

I often wonder what we communicate to the Lord when we have no time for the secret place. It would not take much to discover that our world is filled with people who are in marriage relationships but have no intimacy. If people were committed to what true intimacy requires, then perhaps the divorce rate in our country would fall drastically. If the goal in a marriage was to become more and more intimate with one's spouse, I could guarantee the result would be marriages that are unshakable, joyful and fully satisfying. I believe that at the root of all marriage problems stems some sort of disconnect in the area of intimacy. Can that same disconnect be present in the church today? Do we have pews filled with people who are in relationship with Jesus Christ and yet are not intimately connected with Him?

It is one thing for us to pray and spend time in God's word, but intimacy in the secret place goes far beyond the devotional life. One man whom I have come to admire greatly has significantly taught me about the value of the secret life. I met this pastor and friend several years ago when he had facilitated a silent prayer retreat which I attended for the first time. In the short weekend of being introduced to his passion for the secret life, he made a lasting impression and gave me a greater understanding of what it means to experience intimacy with the Lord. As God would have it, I later joined him to serve in ministry together. I found what this man taught me, several years ago, about the value of being alone with God is still an ever-increasing passion in his life. He is one of the few people I personally know that lives out the pursuit of the secret life. He has imparted in me the need to create an environment in order to cultivate a secret place within the context of my daily life. Although I do not see him as often as I would desire to, he never ceases to encourage me in the pursuit towards intimacy with my God.

E.M. Bounds, a man of the past who also exemplified the secret life, points to the reason why we do not pursue the kind of intimacy that drives us to the art of living the secret life of a worshiper. It comes down to our lack of *desire*. For Bounds, the "deeper the desire," the more driven we are towards the secret life. If we are to experience a living knowledge of our salvation then it is reflected through a desire for the secret life. "Physical appetites are the attributes of a living body, not of a corpse, and spiritual desires belong to a soul made alive to God,"[21] as Bounds compares, and adds:

> A lack of ardor in prayer is the sure sign of a lack of depth and intensity of desire; and the absence of intense desire is a sure sign of God's absence from the heart! To abate fervor is to retire from God. He can, and does, tolerate many things in the way of infirmity and error in his children . . . but two things are intolerable to him—insincerity and

luke warmness. Lack of heart and lack of heat are
two things he loathes"[22]

If we have no desire for the secret, intimate relationship we
are privileged to have with the Lord through Christ, then it
overwhelmingly speaks to the condition of our heart in regards
to our worship.

Consider Jesus' words in the Sermon on the Mount:

> *But when you pray, go into your room, close the*
> *door and pray to your Father who is unseen. Then*
> *your Father who sees what is done in secret, will*
> *reward you"* (Matthew 6:6).

The beauty contained in the secret life of a worshiper is
revealed. This portion of Christ's teaching is at the midway point
of Matthew's record of the sermon. With the entire sermon
essentially focusing upon the kind of life which a disciple is
expected to live, I find it interesting that the teaching on prayer
remains in the middle. It is as if Jesus is suggesting prayer is
the glue that makes everything He is trying to convey stick to
our lives. In Matthew chapter six, Jesus paints a picture of the
contrasting actions between the pagans, religious, and true
worshipers. For the true worshiper, Jesus continually promotes
the idea of a secret life where the worshiper is content on only
having validation and recognition from God. The one who goes
to the secret place for intimacy with the Father is fully satisfied
and is not interested in finding fulfillment in any other place.

In frequenting the secret place, the worshiper is given the
reward of intimacy: life! Jesus came to "give us life" and offers
those who have this secret life the ability to apprehend the coveted
keys to the kingdom of God. If we persist to find fulfillment in any
other place than the secret place of intimacy with the Lord, then
we will only be rewarded with lesser things; however, if we will
"seek first His kingdom and his righteousness" (Matthew 6:33),
then the reality of the living experience of salvation will manifest
itself in our lives. We will access life from the kingdom of God
when we make it our sole desire to pursue intimacy with the Giver

of kingdom life. As you read the biographies of great men and women of God and what they accomplished during their time on earth, they all had a single common thread—intimacy with the Lord in the secret place was their life's priority. The results of what they did because of that secret life was displayed through the incredible accounts of God's power, presence and passion being evident to the world around them.

Brothers and sisters in Christ, is your heart crying out *"Take me away with you—let us hurry! Let the King bring me into his chambers"* (Song of Solomon 1:4)? Our Father in heaven is longing to reward you with a living experience of what the life of salvation is to be. His desire—His sole desire—is for you to be with Him intimately, passionately and privately. He grieves when we desire the lesser things of this life, attempting to satisfy ourselves apart from what only He can give us. If we are to return to a place of worshiping the Father in spirit and in truth, then we must once again do what all true worshipers have come to discover—it is only in the secret place where the life that accompanies our salvation can be birthed and made alive in us!

Chapter Nine

Becoming a Desperate Crumb Licker

*'Yes Lord,' she said, 'but even the dogs eat the
crumbs that fall from their masters' table.'*
Matthew 15:27

*Better is one day in your courts than a thousand
elsewhere; I would rather be a doorkeeper in
the house of my God than dwell in the tents
of the wicked.*
Psalm 84:10

As of late in the Walls household, my seven year old has
developed a nasty habit. On any given day, you can find him
scavenging throughout the kitchen and dining room picking up
any morsel of food that might be present on the countertops
as well as on the floor. To my defense, I can testify that my
children are fed a reasonable amount of food throughout the
day; however, when my son thinks he is starving, he will stop at
nothing to find whatever he can in the way of food to sooth his
hunger pangs. Although I no longer have a dog in my home that
was well trained to double as a broom and mop, I now have a
child who has the potential to eat me out of house and home if I
were to allow him the opportunity.

What if the above story had a few details that were changed? If I were to present it in such a way where I stated that I had no food in my home and my seven year-old was starving; we would not find his behavior humorous or bizarre. The desperate measures which desperate people take never surprise us. We may not always agree with what some people choose to do when faced with an overwhelming crisis, but there is a side of human nature we all can relate with by saying, "I can understand why you felt like you had to do something." It would not be beneath me to find food wherever I could if my children's lives depended upon it. For the sake of survival, my desperation would not hinder my willingness to be humiliated for that which I truly needed. When it comes to those times in our lives, we cannot afford to be picky. Instead, most of us would be extremely grateful to receive any help offered—especially if it was a matter of life or death.

How desperate are you for God? I ask this because I fear that we have lost the kind of desperation for the Lord that is so essential in discovering the radical life of worshiping Him in spirit and in truth. I wonder how many of us would actually take whatever God would offer us. Many in the church believe that we can dictate to God the things that He needs to bestow upon us in the way of His blessings. Call it what you want, but the *name it claim it, blab it grab it, or 58 Days Seed Covenant* approach to God is nothing more than spitting on the face of Christ and cheapening His glorious sacrifice. It's detestable to consider that some see Christ's death as a service to feed our egotistical, selfish desires!

Don't get me wrong, God longs to bless His children. He wants them to eat at the table of His delights and experience the abundant outpouring of His love. But as His children, we do not have the right to decide what we will be served at the master's table; and like a perfect parent He reserves the right to choose what, when, how and where those things will be given in order to benefit our lives in the best way. Understanding this is necessary if we are to return to a genuine worship that seeks the Father in spirit and in truth.

To best illustrate the desperate life that is willing to take what it is given, we reflect upon a conversation between Jesus and a pagan Gentile woman. On the heels of several events in which

Jesus desires to withdraw to a place of solitude (Matthew 13-15, Mark 6-7 and John 6), He is approached by a desperate woman who throws herself at His feet. Jesus' need to withdraw to solitude is significant in understanding the powerful conversation with the woman. Several times before this event, Jesus is challenged with the anemic faith of His followers. Although He understood the weaknesses of humanity, I believe that at times Jesus was frustrated. Consider these events that happened prior to his encounter with the Gentile woman:

- Jesus returned to His hometown of Nazareth where He is ridiculed, rejected and restricted to do what He desired to do (Mark 6:1-6).

- At the time, John the Baptist was beheaded (Matthew 14:1-12). Although John had pointed his followers to Jesus telling them He was the way, John's disciples were still reluctant to follow Jesus (Mark 2:18-22, Matthew 11:1-3).

- Jesus feeds 5,000 people from a few loaves and fishes; however, we find that many of these disciples turn away from Him because they miss the point of what He was trying to reveal about Himself (John 6:25-66).

- Jesus walks on water and His closest friends do not recognize Him and their faith remains weak (Matthew 14:25-31).

- Jesus confronts the religious leaders of His day as they fail to see the dynamic of the spirit of religion versus the spirit of truth (Matthew 15:1-20).

The people who followed Jesus around day after day, challenged by His teaching and awed by His miracles, continually struggled with unbelief. I can almost hear Jesus saying, "How much more do I need to do for you to get the point? I can't take another minute of your chronic fickleness! I need to get away—from you!"

83

Fortunately for us, this is not the case. Instead, in the most unlikely of places and in the most unlikely of people, we see a light bulb going on and the revelation of God's truth being made known. In Matthew 15:21-28 we discover a story where a Gentile woman is commended for her faith; consequently, her faith speaks of something even greater for us to consider—her posture of worship. Although not much is known about this woman, both Matthew and Mark shed light on an important part of the story. Mark's account describes the woman as a "Syrophonecian." Matthew, however, gives a more dramatic nuance to the account by calling her a "Canaanite." Matthew's designation for the woman is the key to understanding the dynamics of the story. For the Jew, the Canaanites represented the most hated people group among their enemies. Mark's gospel, written to Gentiles, describes her simply as a Gentile woman like his audience (Mark 7:26). Matthew's Jewish audience would have seen the story in a much different light. For them, the Canaanite woman was the most unlikely person to be commended by the Lord.

As we place ourselves in this story, picture Jesus as He walks along with His Jewish disciples. He tries to contain a huge smile as this woman, who is absolutely hopeless and worthless in the eyes of those following Him, cries out, "Lord, Son of David, have mercy on me!" His disciples' response is typical. Jesus didn't answer, so they assumed what every other first century Jew would have assumed about the Canaanites: "you are beneath me and you have no business approaching me!" As the woman came running toward and shouting at Jesus, they literally implore Jesus to send her away (v.23). It isn't a matter of them going to Jesus and asking Him, "Lord, should we send her away so she doesn't bother you?" No, the conversation in the modern day vernacular sounds more like, "Jesus, get this woman out of here now! Please, Jesus, we beg you to command this piece of filth to get far away from us!" I have seen a flawed recreation of this story where the disciples are portrayed with smiles in their faces and excited because Jesus was about to do another *miracle*. This picture could not be farther from the truth.

Jews did not associate with Canaanites, and beyond that they did not give the time of day to Gentile women! Before this encounter, Jesus just finished giving a lesson on the difference between the *"clean and unclean"* and He had to insert a, *"Are you still so dull?"* to His disciples (Matthew 15:16). In other words, they weren't getting it. The disciples' opposition to the woman was perfectly natural as they wanted to ensure that their Master would in no way become *unclean* by the encounter.

Take a moment and put yourself in her shoes, get a good picture of the potentially hostile environment she was about to enter. Picture a room full of your worst enemies, and by entering that room you would for certain be making a public spectacle of yourself. Even worse, you have to walk up to the guest of honor and act like a *fool* in order to be acknowledged. To top off the humiliating experience, you would have to paint the quintessential picture of *eating crow* in denying what you believe in favor of accepting what your enemies believe.

"Lord, Son of David, have mercy on me!" was the cry of a desperate Canaanite woman, and yet the loving Jesus says nothing in return. Before we question the compassion of Jesus or dismiss this as the woman simply needing more *faith*, we need to consider why she chose the words that she did. Her designation for Jesus as being "Son of David" was completely out of line for a Canaanite. She wasn't acknowledging that she knew Jesus was indeed the *Messiah* but that He was the Messiah of Israel. As Alfred Edersheim notes, "Spoken by a heathen, these words were an appeal, not to the Messiah of Israel, but to an Israelitish Messiah—for David never reigned over her or her people."[23] Somewhere between her acknowledgment and her beliefs there was a disconnection in her thinking. She knew Him to be messiah-like but she did not actually know Him as the Messiah.

How often does this happen to us? We come to Jesus in the midst of a crisis and we know that He has the ability to change our circumstance; yet we do not see Him for who He truly is. We've acknowledged His Messiah-like qualities in our lives—His salvation, healing and provision—but there are areas of our life that have no concept of a Messiah. Like the Canaanite woman, we find ourselves seeking the hand of Jesus rather than seeking His face. We have a need and we expect Jesus to provide for that need. Because we've heard that Jesus is able to help us, we assume that He will help us regardless of His place in our lives. We can stand in church on Sunday mornings giving Him praise for being our *Lord, King, Father,* and *Savior,* and yet hold on to beliefs that are totally contrary to those claims. We act as if God is obligated to answer us when we call Him even though we do not believe Him to be the Person He is. It's giving Him *lip service* for an hour a week in order to help us feel a little bit better about ourselves the rest for the week. Like the Canaanite woman, we shout out His Name, but in reality, the person behind that Name is completely foreign to us. The Canaanite woman soon learned something in her initial attempt to get Jesus' attention: God cannot be approached on the basis of what we know about Him, but He must be approached by the reality of who He is to us.

She continued to cry after Him but to no avail. After refusing His disciples' request to "send her away," He replies to her cries by stating, *"I was sent only to the lost sheep of Israel"* (Matthew 15:24). In the context of "Lord, Son of David," He was sent only to Israel. Jesus, in a polite way, is asking her, "Why are you, a Canaanite, coming to Me, the Messiah of the Jews? If I am only the Son of David to you, then why are you asking me?" The irony in all of this is that in the previous confrontations between Jesus and the Pharisees, a pagan recognizes something in Jesus which His own people had failed to see. The Jews who saw themselves as being the *clean ones* are being shown their uncleanliness. The clean ones are not those who appear to be clean, but those who show their cleanliness through what they say and do.

The desperate woman now changes her approach. Rather than calling out for His help and bringing attention to the fact that she has no right to appeal to Him based on His *Messiahship,* she attempts to behave in a more appropriate manner. She *"knelt [worshiped] before Him"* and said, *"Lord, help me!"* (Matthew 15:25). This act of humility opened her eyes to the truth that worship begins with submission to the authority of the Lord. Although she could not come to Him on the basis of who He was to someone else, she recognized the fact that Jesus had an authority that went beyond her own. She now calls Him "Lord" and drops the title "Son of David." To solidify her reverence and respect, she approached Jesus in a posture of worship by falling at His feet.

Genuine worship confronts the issue of authority in our lives. Our choice will determine if we will find ourselves being *hand-seekers* or *face-seekers* of the Lord. The Canaanite's initial request was for Jesus to have "mercy" and to "heal" her daughter. Her next request was a more personal acknowledgment saying, "Lord, help me!" There is a world of difference in approaching the Lord by requesting the Lord to *do something for me* versus *do something in me.* When God is only seen as the One who does things for us, we have no concern for His authority over our lives. We certainly respect His power and abilities to intervene into our situation, but we tend to see it as more of a service to us based on the fact that *it's just what He does.*

At the end of her rope, the Canaanite woman knew there was absolutely nothing she could do to make a difference in her situation but to throw herself at the mercy and authority of Jesus. She tried once again and was confronted with the implications of bowing to His Lordship. On the surface, Jesus' response, *"It is not right to take the children's bread and toss it to their dogs"* (v.26) seems to be rather cruel. We have a desperate woman whose daughter is dying, and Jesus is calling her a "dog." In actuality, Jesus was vividly explaining, "because of who you are, I cannot do anything for you." She had come to recognize that Jesus was someone special as a Messiah-like figure and He alone possessed a special authority to meet the needs of people, but it was not enough.

I cannot begin to imagine if Jesus were to say something like this in the context of the modern day church setting. How offensive! How ungrace-like! How pharisaical! However, it is the truth. This is where many in church find their lives today. We come to see Jesus as Savior and recognize the authority He holds as God's Son. Our worship of Him is based on who He is and we celebrate all of the incredible attributes that our God possesses. Sadly, we fail to see that worship must encompass something much more than knowing about God. Seldom do we explore what is necessary to touch the heart of God. Like Colonel Jessup's famous line from *A Few Good Men,* "You want the truth?

You can't handle the truth!" we think we know what it takes to get there; but if we were to dig deeper, we would discover that we are far from the heart of God.

It wasn't enough for the woman to simply recognize who Jesus was—she had to come to recognize who she was! She appealed to Him in every way she could, and finally, Jesus gave her a crushing blow by reminding her, "You do not deserve anything that I have to offer." Can we for one moment come back to that place? Have we forgotten that we deserve absolutely nothing except the fires of Hell from the Lord? Is it now beyond us to think that we are worse than "dogs" in comparison to who He is? What have we done with the truth? Modern day belief suggests sinners and saints alike should feel at ease in the company of a loving Jesus. We make Christ out to be a God who is only concerned with us seeing Him as the One who saves us and cares about us. We have no problem handling those truths. What we do have a difficult time handling is the truth about ourselves! Genuine worship can never take place if we do not first realize the truth about ourselves as compared to the One we are worshipping. Hear His voice even now echoing:

> *It's not right to take the children's bread and toss*
> *it to their dogs.*

The question remains, what will we do with that statement?

The rich young ruler in Mark 10:17-22 had his opportunity to answer that question. He knew about God and he knew what God required of him for worship. Jesus, however, exposed the truth that the young man was not yet a worshiper by any means. Jesus probed the man's heart and revealed the same flaw that is present in today's church: we're happy to worship a God who we know but we will not let the God we worship tell us who we are. The result is that we worship God based on a half-truth that promotes an "I'm okay, you're okay" kind of theology.

The Canaanite woman, however, did the astounding! Rather than being offended by the truth about herself, she did what all true worshipers are prone to do—she humbled herself. She went from calling Jesus the "Son of David" to "Lord" and now He had become "Master." Her reply:

*Yes Lord . . . but even the dogs eat the crumbs that
fall from their master's table.*

gives us a picture of worship. By accepting truth about herself and her place before the Lord, she is saying to Jesus, "I accept the truth of what you are saying about me and I deserve nothing." In her humility, she realized that she did not deserve a place at the table of the Master based upon who she was. She would never see herself as a worthy child, yet despite that, she makes an astonishing request: I want to be a *crumb licker* and would be overwhelmingly grateful for whatever Jesus could offer me! This is humility *par excellence*! Is there any greater condition of the heart than in coming to Jesus saying, "I see my place when it comes to You and I see You as You are and I see me as I am?" The Bible has a phrase for this crumb licking attitude towards worship—it's called coming to the *throne of grace*!

Without coming to an understanding of who we are, we can never come to appreciate or accept the grace of God. One can never know true hope unless they have been in a place of hopelessness. One can never know true love unless they have been unloved. One can never know forgiveness unless they have committed an offense. And in the case of grace, one can never come to receive God's unmerited favor in such a way that would cause one to be drawn to the heart of God unless they have seen themselves as undeserving to be in the presence of the King. Among all of the underappreciated aspects of God's blessings which He bestows upon man, I believe that grace stands at the forefront of them all.

My beliefs concerning grace will most likely be different than what is commonly understood in the church today. Too many believing Christians see grace as being the proverbial argument for an anti-works view of salvation. While Ephesians 2:8 tells us that our salvation is an act of God's grace in that there is absolutely nothing we can do by the way of works to obtain it, the meaning and function of grace goes far beyond that reasoning.

Unfortunately, grace is equated with a misguided idea of God's permissiveness when it comes to our sin and failure. Many tend to hold the belief that God accepts our imperfections and no longer holds a standard of holiness over our lives, seeing it as *legalism* or *pharisaicalism.*

This is best exemplified in what we have done with John 3:16. We tend to see *"For God so loved the world that he gave"* to mean that God's love for us equals God's pleasure in us. His grace becomes this intangible reality which is an endless supply of His favor upon us despite the life we choose to live. We dare not say to a brother or sister in Christ that they are somehow not in line with obeying God's Word. Doing that would be stepping over the line of grace and violating the John 3:16 principle that God loves them. After all, in our society we believe it is impossible to reject a person's beliefs and actions while at the same time say that we "love them."

But if God's grace is so abundant and it doesn't matter where we are in life as His *grace is enough,* then why didn't Jesus immediately respond to the Canaanite woman? Why would He make her feel as if she didn't deserve what she was asking? Certainly, Jesus was never harsh with the sinners like He was the religious leaders. He embraced all of them and doted over their harmless imperfections, while by His grace, He was able to overlook all of their sinful ways—at least that's how it is described in many of our churches today.

The truth of the matter was that the Canaanite woman was in a place where she could not yet receive the grace of God. This is what has been lost in our picture of His grace. It is often seen as a permission slip for failure in our walk of faith. And when our actions and attitudes do not line up with the truth of His Word, we proudly pull out the grace card to justify our behavior. We act as if we deserve His grace, and see His unmerited favor as something that is merited in our minds.

The idea of coming to the throne of grace needs to be prefaced with the posture of humility and gratitude. The *"confidence"* or *"boldness"* (Hebrews 10) we have in coming to the throne of grace does not stem from an attitude of entitlement. It is a freedom from the fear of God's wrath and a cheerful assurance that we have been welcomed into His presence. It has nothing to do with our *right* but everything to do with our *privilege.* The Canaanite woman was given a privilege she did not deserve. She was able to receive the favor and blessing from a Messiah who was not rightfully hers. Initially when we experience God's grace in our salvation, we have the right posture before the throne; however, something happens over time and what was once a precious keepsake is now common.

Imagine an encounter between Jesus and the Canaanite woman in our modern day setting after she embraces today's view of grace. She had received His grace and had bowed at the Master's feet and worshiped Him. But now that she has "tasted and seen that the Lord is good," she figures that Jesus can do more in her life in the form of blessings. Rather than crying out to Him, "Lord, Son of David, have mercy," she casually strolls up to Jesus and says, "Hey, I need to be provided for. You did this before in my life and I know that I can count on Your support this time as well. In fact Lord, because You did this for me in the past and I noticed that Your Word says You do this kind of thing all of the time, then I guess You need to keep Your promises and do it for me again."

In many ways, we approach the Lord in the same way. We use His Word and His promises as a standard against Him. We act as if we belong in the throne room of His presence instead of being recipients of an invitation which we did not deserve to be given. Humility has become a tool to use so that God will "lift us up" rather than a way of life that says, "I'm satisfied with the Master's crumbs." David said it best in Psalm 84:10 when he expressed the depths of privilege he felt in simply being able to be in the presence of the Lord to worship Him:

> *Better is one day in your courts than a thousand elsewhere; I would rather be a doorkeeper in the house of my God than dwell in the tents of the wicked* (Psalm 84:10).

David displayed the humility of feeling that he did not have the right to be in the house of the Lord and the gratitude of partaking of God's presence in any form or fashion.

God's bestowal of His grace upon us is not something we should casually accept; however, because we have lost the sense of humility and gratitude, we have also lost the intended impact of grace upon our worship. When God directs His unmerited favor towards our lives, our response should be one of overwhelming gratitude. Humility is the attitude that fuels gratitude. It's picturing ourselves the way we truly are without the intervention of Christ's work on the cross and realizing that we do not even deserve to lick the crumbs off the floor around the Master's table. It's great to realize who we are in Christ, but don't ever forget, we deserve none of it. Until we reach the point of returning to a place of humility and gratitude in our worship, we will never come to experience the true heart of the Father.

We need to recapture a genuine understanding of grace if we are to return to the place of worshiping the Father in spirit and in truth. Every time we open His Word, we are experiencing *grace*—even when it says, "Thou shall not!" Every time we utter a prayer, we are experiencing *grace*. Every time His Spirit brings conviction to our lives, we are experiencing *grace*. Grace is not an excuse for failing to live for Christ and obeying His Word. Grace is what empowers us to freely live for Christ in every area of our lives. Grace is like the Canaanite woman who understood her place in the presence of Christ. When she realized she did not deserve to even capture His attention, something incredible happened. The favor of God came upon her life, and she went from knowing about the Messiah to actually experiencing His love and power. This is the beauty of grace. It is not earned, but it is sought after through the walk of humility and gratitude. And just as a pagan Gentile woman became an example to those who supposedly knew the truth about the Messiah, grace allows us to behold what others are missing—the unprecedented favor of God on our lives, and the understanding that those who have made themselves "least" by becoming desperate crumb lickers under the King's table are the ones who actually feast with the King "face to face."

As I bow at Your feet
Lord I know I don't belong
Still You remain ever faithful to me
You lift me up when I'm humbled on my knees
(Lyrics from *More* by Jay Walls)

Chapter Ten

Worship in the Fast Lane

You cannot fast as you do today and expect your
voice to be heard on high.
Isaiah 58:4

Is not this the kind of fasting I have chosen:
to loose the chains of injustice and untie the cords
of the yoke, to set the oppressed free and
break every yoke?
Isaiah 58:6

I have to make an honest confession. When I sit in some churches I feel absolutely suffocated by all that is going on. It is as if a pillow is being smothered on my face, holding me down as I try to gasp for a single breath. I have never taken amphetamines, but at times I wonder if many of our worship services suffer from an addiction to *speed*.

Growing up, I hated rollercoasters; however, I loved anything that would spin me around to the point where it felt like I wasn't going to be able to walk straight for a week. As I have gotten older, I have come to a startling discovery—I can no longer take the constant motion of spinning around! The resulting migraine, nausea and stiff neck have made me a huge fan of the simpler things in life. And like a mature adult who can no longer take the gravitational forces of amusement park rides, I have come to a place where I can no longer stomach the repetitive, going through the motions, theme park worship setting in the church today. As an occasional participant, I have to ask myself as I did when I stopped going to the theme park, "What's the point?"

What is the point of what we do in our worship service today? Why do we sing the songs that we do, and why do we go to such great lengths to execute every element of the service to flawless perfection? Maybe when the band strikes the last chord and the preacher has articulated his final point, we are able to all go out the church doors exclaiming "WOW! I can't wait to get back on this ride next time!" We hail the creativity of our services filled with the latest music, riveting dramas, state of the art videos, and of course, a relevant, felt-needs message that is sure to keep you wanting to come back for more. But at the end of the day, what has really changed? Sure, we've gone through Sunday's religious ritual with excellence and have found a way to captivate the local audience, but when the curtain closes has anything really changed?

It seems that many of our worship leaders in the local church spend more time emulating the latest *professional* worship leaders by trying to mimic every nuance of their latest songs. Rather than striving for a worship set that is Spirit-led and aims to lead people to the throne room of God, their concern is in replicating the performance of the recording artist. As a worship leader, I hear arguments such as, "We're doing this for the Lord! If the world does things with excellence, so should we!" While excellence is not to be ignored, we need to ask: "Whose standard of excellence are we pursuing?" I'm sure that when Paul said, "Be excellent in all you do," he would have preferred that those involved in the worship ministry excel in prayer and the spiritual disciplines rather than being able to perfect the latest guitar lick that would send the song *over the top*. As good as the modern day worship experience looks and sounds, if it is truly making an impact, then why does it seem as if things remain the same week in and week out? Where are the changed lives? Where are the healings? Where are the Christians being *sent out* with power from the Sunday service to impact the world around them?

The answer is simple: We've come to accept worship in the fast lane—more energy, more drama, more technology and more creativity which drives worship to being an event of captivation for spiritual thrill seekers. And just as it is so easy to race to the amusement park and enjoy the rides without even thinking about the hundreds of people you pass who are not as fortunate as you, we have missed the bigger thrill along the way—giving those less fortunate a taste of what we have taken for granted.

The Spirit of religion reigns when worship becomes solely about the worshiper. Religion seeks only to serve the individual and not the God of the individual. When it comes to this in our worship, the greater blessings of God are missed and the overall power of the church is diminished. We have what we consider *great worship* in the church but in the end, if it only results in an introverted experience of our faith, then in essence, our expressions of worship means nothing. It has not changed us enough to change the world around us.

In many ways, the religious rituals hailed by the religious community of the Old Testament are approached the same way as our churches today. Striving for *par excellence* has developed an attitude that we can do certain things to enhance our worship in order to produce a greater worship experience. While it seems that we have equated excellence with *righteousness,* we have failed to see that modeling certain religious behaviors in view of the public's eye does not necessarily communicate acts of righteous worship before the Lord. Muddled in this perspective is the inability to distinguish between the heart of worship and the actions of worship. The prophet Isaiah saw this in his own day as he prophesied to his people:

> *"Is this the kind of fast I have chosen, only a day for*
> *people to humble themselves? Is it only for bowing*
> *one's head like a reed and for lying in sackcloth and*
> *ashes? Is that what you call a fast, a day acceptable*
> *to the LORD [emphasis added]?"* (Isaiah 58:5)

Isaiah 58 began the prophet's emphasis upon the eschatological events of Zion's everlasting deliverance and the everlasting judgment of her enemies. But before Isaiah could address Israel's future promise of hope, he had to deliver a word of correction concerning the lack of genuine worship in which the people of God had been found guilty. Upon the heels of a message of hope that focused on Yahweh's intervention of healing and restoration (Isaiah 57:14-21), Isaiah turned his attention to the people's failure to "do righteousness" as depicted in their "selfish and oppressive" behavior.[24] Initially, the words of the prophet in Isaiah 58 appeared to be sympathetic towards the suffering people. They seemed eager to know the ways of God and to show their commitment to Yahweh; they began to fast.

For most of us, we know that *fasting* can be a profitable spiritual discipline that enriches our walk with the Lord. It offers a small token of sacrifice in denying our flesh for the sake of drawing nearer to the heart of God. In Isaiah 58, however, the people's choice to fast as opposed to offering prayer and sacrifice as a means to seek the Lord, is telling of their sinful condition. Historically, Israel was called to fast once a year for the Day of Atonement (Leviticus 23:26-32). Although there were other instances in which fasting was called for by Israel's leaders (e.g. 2 Chr. 20:3, Ezra 8:23, Esther 4:16), fasting to influence a deity to intervene on behalf of the people was a common practice among the pagan nations.[25] One such practice in the Canaanite religion was to fast in order to put the gods under pressure to perform for them.[26] God's accusations (Isaiah 58:3-5) against His people were not over the act of fasting; rather, God condemned their attempt to *manipulate* their worship in order to obtain His favor.

The first of these accusations assumed the sin of idolatry. The people had put forth an exaggerated display of religious ritual in the attempt to manipulate Yahweh in the same manner as any common god of the surrounding nations. Israel's desire for the Lord to serve their purposes reduced Him to what other nations believed their idols did on behalf of their religious manipulations. They did not intend for Yahweh to see through the motives of their hearts and to expose their selfish and oppressive ways.

The second accusation Yahweh cited was Israel's failure to exercise justice. The prophet established that one of the foundational elements of acceptable worship is to "maintain justice" (Isaiah 56:1). In Biblical thought, justice is closely identified with the idea of righteousness. Where righteousness strives for "conformity to God's ways" especially in regards to "ethical behavior," justice can be seen as the "manner, custom or way of living under" the demands of the "moral law."[27] Isaiah revealed that the people had exploited their workers. He further insinuated that they disobeyed the covenant by failing to meet the needs of the hungry, shelter the alien and clothe the naked (Isaiah 58:7). The failure to exercise justice was not only a sin against their fellow man but also against God. In Abraham Heschel's *The Prophets*, he notes that justice is more than a moral value to be exercised in the relationship between man and man; rather, "it is an act of God" reflective of not just one of His ways but "all His ways."[28]

The third accusation contained in Isaiah's declaration is the root cause of the people's dilemma: selfishness. Isaiah used the phrase *"do as you please"* (Isaiah 58:3, 13) to reveal the condition of the people's hearts as being an offense to Yahweh as they endeavored to worship Him. The motive for all they had done was not based on a sincere desire to please the Lord but for the sake of serving themselves.[29] By exploiting their workers, refusing to feed the hungry, failing to shelter the homeless and neglecting to clothe the naked, the people stood exposed of their greed and unconcern. Isaiah mocked their selfishness in condemning the fact that their fasting, intending to draw them nearer to God, had *"brought out the worst in the human spirit"* (Isaiah 58:4).[30] The actions of the people testified against them revealing the lack of righteous living that had been commanded. From all that Isaiah had charged against them, the people stood guilty of violating the covenant through their unrighteous actions towards God and one another.

In the attempts to secure freedom from their oppressors by fasting, they had become further bound in their sin. In an answer to the rhetorical question of Isaiah 58:6, the prophet submitted the idea that if the people had been truly fasting, the results would have empowered them, blessed them and brought the favor of the Lord upon them. Dallas Willard comments on the idea that the practice of true fasting is something which will result in "aiding life in vital interaction with the Kingdom of God"; however, because Israel abused the essence of true fasting, it became a "useless or even harmful exercise in religion."[31] Isaiah's words reminded the people that true spiritual worship is not reflected in the actions of religious rituals but by the fruit that comes forth from those actions. Had they been exercising righteousness as a way of life, the proof of the Lord's favor would have been evident upon their lives. Isaiah 58 serves as a poignant reminder that worship is not an expression of one's *religion* but a reflection of one's *heart*.

Within the myriad of theological differences contained in the guise of the Christian faith, something has been lost in the majority of churches—a genuine worship that expresses itself in the righteous actions of God's people. Perhaps we have become a society of believers that have chosen a faith that best suits our needs; one in which we can control and manipulate so that it will not require the sacrificial life of discipleship but still retain our place in heaven.

Worship in the fast lane is a dangerous place to be. By focusing intently on *how* we are doing worship rather than *why* we are doing worship places us in the world of Isaiah 58. With all that we are doing in the worship services, have we forgotten the bigger picture that screams out to us: There is something much more than ourselves! We can continue to live under the impression that we are touching the heart of God, when in reality, if through our lives His heart is not touching those around us—the sick, the poor, the lonely, the afflicted and the oppressed—we've missed the exit to where the ride of worship was intended to take us. Do we truly believe that God is pleased with all of the noise and clatter that does nothing more than make us say, "Worship was awesome"? Isn't God the one who should be noticed? If all that we are doing is producing an environment where people are happy to come to church, we've missed the point.

God's people in Jerusalem during Isaiah's day felt as if they were accomplishing something great by their habitual fasting. And just as there is *nothing new under the sun*, we tend to step back and relish the heights of a worship experience that serves to make us feel better about ourselves and our church. The real question mimics that of the prophet's:

> Is this the kind of worship which I have chosen? That a man would delight himself for a Sunday in the midst of exceptional music, professional multi-media, riveting drama, and relevant felt-needs messages in order to sing the praises of his church and be wowed in the name of excellence?

Our music, preaching and creativity mean nothing unless they result in a *life* of worship that walks in obedience to God. We can pretend our attempt to perfect the worship service is doing something significant, but unless it is changing lives in the church and impacting the world around us, we're simply practicing idolatry, callousness and selfishness. And just like the prophet Isaiah, I will *"shout it aloud"* and *"raise my voice like a trumpet"* to declare that the day of introverted, self-centered, amusement-based worship practices must come to an end as they are not acceptable to the Lord! We need to return to the heart of worship in order to restore us to the purposes of God. We are to finish the work the Lord began while we wait for our day of deliverance—and that work is to live out our worship in a way that transforms the world in which we live:

> *"The Spirit of the Lord is on me, because He has anointed me to proclaim good news to the poor. He has sent me to proclaim freedom for the prisoners and recovery of sight for the blind, to set the oppressed free, to proclaim the year of the Lord's favor."* (Luke 4:18-19)

Chapter Eleven

A Return to the Beginning

All of them were filled with the Holy Spirit . . .
Acts 2:4

*Now the Lord is the Spirit, and where the Spirit of
the Lord is, there is freedom.*
2 Corinthians 3:17

When it comes to driving and directions, I seldom find myself saying, "I have absolutely no clue where I am or where I am going." Although I will not go as far as boasting about my uncanny ability to navigate to various locations, I will submit that I do have a great sense of direction. Every once in a while, however, I find myself scratching my head saying, "I think somewhere along the way, I must have made a wrong turn." One thing I have learned is that if I return to a familiar place and start over, I can usually find my way to the place I want to go.

God has given the church specific directions as to where we need to go on the journey of worship. Certainly, the Word of God is a more than adequate as a roadmap providing perfect directions. The problem is we have failed to read the map properly and have neglected to stay on the proper route. It seems that the church stands at a crossroad of unmarked territory far from the destination God intends for us to be. We are off the map and

103

in our stubbornness we are acting as if we know exactly where to go.

In considering the approach to worship in our modern day mindset, I am reminded of a scene from my favorite musical *The Fiddler on the Roof.* The story emphasizes one man's struggle to balance the idea of "tradition" and a world that is quickly changing around him. In the opening song, *Tradition*, the main character, Tevye, begins to boast about the traditions of the Jewish people. He describes the prayer tassels that hang from his garment and poses the question to the effect of, "And do you know where we got this tradition? I'll tell you" and after a brief pause he answers, "I don't know." I would be willing to bet that if the same question was asked to the church today in regards to their worship practices, we would respond much like Tevye. We could explain what we're doing and what the various elements of our worship are for, but I believe that we would fail to answer the question of, "Why we do what we do?"

Like Tevye, we follow a roadmap of our worship traditions. Regardless of how old or new those traditions may be, it seems when confronted with the reality of where the road is leading us, even though they are familiar roads, we will simply throw our hands up in the air and declare, "We have no idea where all of this is going." We go through the rituals of worship and even experience a driving momentum which corporate worship can bring to the Body of Christ; yet when it comes to where the destination of worship is to lead us, we appear to be lost on the road of destiny as poor wandering beggars who cannot find their way.

Worship does have a destination. If done in the context of spirit and truth, we should always arrive at the exact same place each time we embark upon the worship journey. There is no new revelation when we worship the Lord, only a timeless revelation that expands endlessly throughout all time and eternity. In worship, God reveals Himself to man and man beholds His God. This privileged, exclusive relationship of the believer is wrapped up in the simplicity of revelation and response. Though a person who has not come to the saving knowledge of Jesus Christ can praise the Lord in recognizing the Creator and His awesome works, the unbeliever is incapable of worship because he lacks the one essential aspect which only the believer can attest—the Spirit of the Living God dwelling within.

Our skewed approach to worship today has caused us to lose sight of the most important thing—the Spirit-filled life—which we have been given access to when we first came to the cross of Christ. The deliberate steps taken by many churches in order to be relevant to the fleshly aspects of our lives, disregard the central goal of worship in connecting our lives with the Spirit of God. A heavy emphasis placed upon connecting with our fellow man and his needs has redirected the focus of the worship from its original intent. These steps have unfortunately caused us to drift from the road laid out before us. Like a person who has discovered that they have strayed from the path, if we are to ever find our way back to worship *in spirit* and *in truth,* we must retrace our steps and return to the beginning of where our journey started.

I am often frustrated when I hear people describe the various reasons why we worship in the church. The ones that bother me the most include the ideas that worship prepares us to hear the Word and worship helps draw people into the presence of God. Generally, people view the song service at a church as a warm-up for the preacher's sermon. Interestingly, modeled in the book of Acts and other places around the world, it is prayer and not worship that prepares the heart for God's word. When God's word is received, then a response of worship follows. Thus, worship doesn't prepare us for the message but rather should come as a response to the message.

The idea that worship draws us into the presence of the Lord is also a misinformed perspective. As believers, we are never far from God's presence. He is not only *around* us but He dwells *in* us. In some ways, we have made worship a mystical transaction of trying to summon the presence of God before us like a genie in a bottle. If we rub the worship lamp extra hard, then perhaps we will come into the presence of God! Nothing could be farther from the truth. When we worship, something happens within us. The reality of God's presence becomes tangible when we magnify His presence in our lives, and in order to do that, He must increase and we must decrease (Mark 3:30). We cannot conjure up the presence of God because He is already in our midst. We can, however, minimize, squelch, ignore and disregard His presence through the activities and focuses of our lives.

In his book *Forgotten God*, Francis Chan writes about a problem the church is facing in its worship practices. Chan's premise is summed up by the following statement:

> From my perspective, the Holy Spirit is tragically neglected and, for all practical purposes, forgotten. While no evangelical would deny His existence, I'm willing to bet there are millions of churchgoers across America who cannot confidently say they have experienced His presence or action in their lives over the past year. And many of them do not believe they can.[32]

The Holy Spirit has become lost in our worship and we desperately need to find Him again! He should be given the liberty to take center stage in our worship services. Instead, we have taken over the platform of worship by developing a culture that makes us feel relaxed with who we are and the God we worship. The problem, however, is in realizing that without the presence of the Holy Spirit, a living and active presence, the church has no identity.

The problem we face with losing our identity stems from our focus as the church. Somewhere along the way, the cross has become the predominate symbol of identification of the church, and this has become the center of worship. For example, in our worship songs we sing about the cross and the more appealing things associated with it—grace, love and salvation. By doing so, we have made the cross a wonderful place of contentment that fails to challenge our lives toward a deeper walk with Christ. We have upheld the idea of the cross of Christ and relished in the victory that His death and sacrifice has brought us; however, if we fail to apprehend the incredible life in the Spirit that was afforded to us by the virtue of the cross, we have done a great injustice in appropriating the work of our Savior.

Today's believers wear the cross proudly around their necks and don T-shirts that have pictures of the cross promoting their identity with Christ. I, however, have concerns as to where this is leading. If the cross was to be at the forefront of our faith, then why did the church have to wait before being commissioned to go forth as the church? After all, the crucifixion was over and Jesus had resurrected—what else did they need? They could have proclaimed, "Jesus died on a cross and spilled His blood to take away our sin!" and proceeded to evangelize the world on that basis. We could declare to the world that the cross reminds us of Jesus' sacrifice and that we, like good followers, are now crucified with Him in His death; but have we considered the many other religions whose participants practice a life of being crucified in their faith? Do we not think that committing suicide by flying a jet into the World Trade Center for the sake of serving Allah is not a form of bearing a cross for the sake of one's religion? For the Christian, something much more radical is required to define our identities as the worshipers of Jesus Christ. And while we should be grateful for the cross and what it has brought to our lives, we are to be defined by something which God sees as the most important part of our identity as worshipers of Christ—the Holy Spirit.

The New Testament accounts of Jesus' post-resurrection activities are interesting to consider. Acts 2:4 states, *"All of them were filled with the Holy Spirit."* Before this happened, the disciples were already *breathed upon* when Jesus said *"Receive the Holy Spirit"* (John 20:22). Why was it necessary that they wait in Jerusalem for the "gift my Father promised?" If they already had received the Holy Spirit in John 20:22, then why did they need to wait to receive Him again? The answer shows the difference between our identity with Christ and our identity with the church.

Currently, I consume about one gallon of water a day; even though I am drinking water, you would not look at me and think, "He's been drinking water today." You would, however, be able to look at someone who is dehydrated and say, "That person needs something to drink!" But if you were to pour a gallon of water over my head and completely drench my body, it would be evident to everyone that I have come in contact with water. Although I had the water inside of me, it was not evident to the world around me. By drenching myself, I have now become identified as being someone who has been covered with water!

Our salvation works the same way. We receive Christ and begin consuming the Living Water. This is what the disciples received in John 20:22 as a result of the death and resurrection of Christ. But this is not enough for the world to stand up and take notice. The Living Water from Jesus is not only meant to be consumed but also poured out upon His people. In turn, this outpouring of the Holy Spirit was for the express purpose to be "witnesses" (Acts 1:8) to the world—in other words, the world would be able to identify the church with Christ through the process of the baptism of the Holy Spirit!

The story of Acts 2 is widely debated and depending on which theological camp you rest in, you believe either you receive it at salvation or an event subsequent to salvation. My personal belief is the latter has the strongest biblical support. The Bible unequivocally submits the idea that something visible, tangible and powerful is inherent to the Holy Spirit's work within the church—otherwise, Acts 2 would not had been a necessary event. If the internal witness of God's Spirit (John 20:22) was enough to ensure the mission, then why was Pentecost recorded in Scripture? The experience of the cross should lead us to the experience of a Pentecost.

Like our salvation, there is evidence which identifies the church with the Holy Spirit. While the believer has an internal evidence of the Spirit such as peace, assurance, faith, hope and joy, the church has the external witness of the Spirit which serves to validate its existence. Although a group of Christians can come together and meet in a building on Sunday, it does not necessarily serve as a witness that God is among them. No offense to my dispensationalist brothers and sisters in Christ, but even if that group is sitting around discussing the Bible, it is not enough witness to validate that the church is identified with Jesus Christ. God has given His church something much more to ensure their witness to the world.

This reality was made evident to me during a revival service when I was eleven-years-old. For most of my young life, I had gone to a variety of churches which, in my opinion, were all the same. You sang some songs, you heard the preacher preach, you prayed and then went home. My family had started attending a new church and my mom had dragged me to a mid-week service. About half-way through the evangelist's message, a blood-curdling shriek came from behind me. Suddenly, a woman swiftly ran by the pew where I was sitting. She was disfigured, pale white and her stomach was convulsing. An intense coldness moved with her as she flailed her arms approaching the platform. As she attempted to attack the evangelist, he authoritatively shouted, "In the name of Jesus, come out of her!" In an instant, she fell as though all life was drained from her. The evangelist reached down, took her hand and helped her up. The woman's countenance had changed and she proceeded to share of her life of bondage to a demon for twenty years—Jesus had set her free. That night, I realized that God was no longer a person that existed in a book or resided in heaven. He was real, He was present and He was powerful!

The gifts of the Spirit were meant to be a vital part of the Spirit's life flowing within the Body of Christ. Some have tried to jump through hermeneutical circles in order to explain away the necessity or existence of spiritual gifts in today's church. In their quest, they have created churches in which the Spirit has not been able to gift them with His presence. This has produced a form of Christianity that attempts to live by the *letter of law* while barring portions of scripture that tell the church of the gifts which God's unchangeable Spirit has given His people. 1 Corinthians 12-14 gives the blueprint for spiritual gifts in the church, and contextually it provides an in-depth study of the nature, function and purposes for the gifts of the Spirit. The Corinthians abused these gifts which gave Paul the occasion to address these issues in Scripture. Paul described a picture of a healthy functioning church evidenced by the presence of the Holy Spirit. This leads us to the problem: where is the evidence of the Holy Spirit in our worship today? If the first church began their existence with the manifest presence and power of God's Spirit being evident not only to the believers but also to the unbelievers who came into contact with the church, why aren't our services filled with the same kind of presence of God's Spirit? Where is His presence that moves beyond the realm of what we feel internally and becomes an external reality to those around us?

The first church of Acts 2 waited in Jerusalem until the promise of the Father was given. In a sense, this was their time in the tomb before being raised in the glory of God on the day of Pentecost. Although the cross became a symbol for the church in that it represented the essence of what gave them salvation, it was the Holy Spirit that testified to their identity with the Spirit of Christ. The goal of Christianity is not to relish in the cross of Christ but to be transformed by His Spirit. The apostle Paul said it best when He declared:

> I have been crucified with Christ and I no longer live,
> but Christ lives in me. The life I live in the body, I live
> by faith in the Son of God, who loved me and gave
> himself for me. (Galatians 2:20)

Paul's perspective is not in identifying himself with the cross of Christ, but he is identified with the life of Christ. The evidence of Paul's faith does not rest upon having Jesus in his life; it rests upon Jesus having Paul's life.

If the church is full of the life of Christ, then we must ask ourselves, "What proves we have that life?" Jesus' testimony of being the One *sent from God* was not based upon His ability to teach others God's Word nor was it because He was crucified. He was identified with the Father because the Spirit of God was demonstrated through His life. Hebrews 2:4, in speaking of the reality of Christ's work, explains that "God also testified to it [salvation] by signs, wonders, and various miracles, and gifts of the Holy Spirit distributed according to His will." If the life of Christ is being displayed within the four walls of the church, then the results would be proven by the manifestation of the Spirit's activity among His people. Paul echoes this idea when he told the Corinthians that it wasn't the "gospel message" that testified to his claims about salvation but it was *"a demonstration of the*

Spirit's power so that your faith might not rest on man's wisdom, but on God's power" (1 Corinthians 2:1-5). We have the message of the cross and the Word of God, but without the power of the Holy Spirit being made known, how are those truths validated?

True worship must be practiced in spirit and in truth. Beyond a theological ascent or knowledge of Biblical truths, true worship also encompasses the intangible—the Spirit. In worship we welcome the presence of an Omnipotent, Omniscient, Transcendent and Supernatural Being to be a guest in the presence of natural, fleeting, weak and powerless people and even then we somehow don't believe something other-worldly should be the result of that encounter. Worship is an activity of the spirit, but we still seem tied to only identifying it with the flesh. We sing about God holding us, embracing us, wiping away our tears and healing our hearts; yet those encounters should also produce an atmosphere where prophesying, speaking in tongues, miracles, physical healings and various other evidences of the Spirit are present in our worship! We have to allow for His Spirit to have the freedom to do what He desires to do in the midst of the church. If worship is something that draws us closer to Christ and in turn makes us more like Christ, then shouldn't the same Spirit which identified Christ with the Father through "signs, wonders, miracles, and the gifts of the Spirit" also be present in a worshiping church?

Somewhere along the way the church has lost its way. It strayed from its initial starting point where a small group of believers sought the Lord in an upper room. Before they embarked upon any missionary journeys, before they evangelized their neighborhoods, before they began open-air crusades and before they felt the need to build multi-million dollar edifices to house the trophies of their *ministry*, they worshiped the Lord until the Spirit of God made His presence known among them. Had that humble beginning never taken place, the church would have ceased to exist! The first church was not defined as the group that believed in the *dead man* on the cross; rather, they were defined as the people who did signs, wonders and miracles in the same power as Jesus. Why do we feel that hanging around the cross is enough for us to exist as the church? If those who forged the way were convinced that they needed to be endued with power by the Spirit, why aren't we convinced of the same?

Today, more than anything, we need a return to the beginning and we are far from it! Sadly, if we look around the church on any given Sunday and listen to the conversations that take place, a startling discovery will be made: people within the four walls of the church do not appear to be living in any more freedom than those who remain in the world. We talk football, entertainment, politics and the latest church gossip; where is the talk that testifies to the power and glory of the Lord taking place in the lives of His people? In our quest to forge our own way of worship, we have strayed from the path of the Spirit. His predominance in the worship experience has been lost in lieu of trying to fit everything we do in a worship service in a span of an hour and fifteen minutes. The waiting upon the Lord modeled in Acts 2 is no longer an option in our society. We are too busy and too preoccupied with the lesser and selfish things of life. We love a worship experience that appeals to our fleshy needs and desires. We want to know that God *loves us* and *embraces us* in our time of need. But that is not enough to bring us to a place of freedom.

When the Spirit of the Lord is present and active among His people, something special transpires. Paul said:

> *Now the Lord is the Spirit, and where the Spirit of*
> *the Lord is, there is freedom* (2 Corinthians 3:17).

We can say, "Jesus has set us free," but the reality of that statement will only exist within the church if the Holy Spirit is able to take center stage in the worship experience. It's great to focus on things like the Lord's Supper and remember what Jesus did on the cross. There is something intimately special when communion is experienced by the body of Christ; but even Jesus made His disciples realize that there was something even greater which they needed if they were to become His church in which the *"gates of hell will not overcome it"* (Matthew 16:18). He wanted them to wait for the Spirit. Without the Spirit, they could do nothing of significance. Without the Spirit, they could not offer a world bound with sin a freedom that would break every fetter. Without the Spirit, they could never fulfill the plan mapped out before them by their Lord and Savior. Yes, they had the Spirit within, but they needed to have Him poured upon and poured forth from their lives as well (Acts 2:1-4). Even Jesus modeled the reality of this experience before He began His ministry (Matthew 1:16, Mark 1:10). Unfortunately, we have come to believe that we are beyond needing such an empowering.

Although I cannot fully address the topic of the Baptism of the Holy Spirit in this book, as it is a controversial subject that is worthy of much discussion, I believe that it is a subsequent (Acts 2:1-4, Acts 8:12-17, and Acts 10) and an on-going (Acts 4:31, 13:52, and Ephesians 5:18) event. We are empowered by the Spirit in order to testify (witness) to the reality of Christ in our lives (Acts 1:8). Jesus displayed power in his ministry that caused people to recognize that what He was doing was not possible in the realm of the natural. He was identified with the Father. The disciples displayed power in their ministry that identified them with Jesus (Acts 4:13). If we have the reality of the outpouring of the Holy Spirit in the church today, where is the power that testifies to that truth? Why aren't people flocking to the church to be healed as opposed to going to the hospital? Why are so many prescribed anti-depressants because they can't cope with life rather than running to the church to be given the power to overcome this world? Does the power we have in the church witness to the world that the church is where the "Spirit of the Lord is?"

The reason we are not winning the lost to Jesus Christ is because we are not offering that which will bring freedom to those who remain in bondage. After all, how can we offer what we do not readily have? Rather than creating an atmosphere where we wait upon the Holy Spirit to be poured out and are sensitive to His leading, we try to make worship something that is attractive to the flesh. And while we keep people attentive and engaged in their pews through our creative efforts, the Spirit remains silent. We preach of how awesome, powerful and necessary God is for our lives, but we dare not give the Spirit the opportunity to demonstrate the reality of who He is and what He has come to do for our lives.

If the command of the Lord to wait in Jerusalem for the gift of the Father was given to us today, I fear that we would be forever waiting to receive anything from the Lord. The saints of old held strongly to the idea of *tarrying*. More than simply being patient and waiting for something to happen, tarrying was an intense laboring in seeking the Lord. There was uncomfortable work involved. To best illustrate this idea, think of a spring of refreshing water buried deep beneath the ground. Those who tarry know that in order to get to the spring, they must pick up a shovel and begin to dig. With each time the spade hits the dirt and with every toss of the shovel over their shoulder, they are tarrying as they wait in expectation for a crystal clear spring to burst forth. In our day, we have no spiritual work ethic. We know the spring is there, but we wait for the excavators to show up with their power equipment to dig the hole for us. We sit around and look at the ground and say, "we're waiting!" The unfortunate truth is that we're content with someone else doing the work for us. After all, no one wants to get dirty and break a sweat. And because we're not exerting the energy necessary to dig the well, we're not thirsty for more. Instead, we're content with digging our own cisterns that are shallow and fail to produce anything significant in our lives (Jeremiah 2:13).

In reflecting back on the story of Jesus and the woman at the well, Jesus made a profound statement. He told the woman that *"if you knew the gift of God and who it is that asks you for a drink, you would of asked him and he would have given you living water"* (John 4:10). Jesus suggested that in the woman's waiting upon Jesus that she *wait* for Him to give her a drink. We often wait *upon* Jesus in our worship and offer Him a drink from our worship. How often do we wait *for* Jesus to give us a drink from the living water? Think about the Samaritan woman. She had to *dig up the dirt* of her life before the Lord could offer her a drink of living water; but the work was worth her effort as she was given freedom! For us, however, we remain content sipping water from the well of regularity and conversing with Jesus. We show up each week to get our jar of water filled and then go on our merry way. Just as the woman was lost and had a misguided journey as to what life was to be, we too are lost in where we have allowed the journey of worship to take us—to wells that can never satisfy the soul.

Rather than keep going, perhaps we need to wait upon the Lord. Like the wayward traveler who thinks he is going the right direction to his destination and yet is miles off course, we need to come to recognize that although we claim we have the *map*, there is a very strong possibility we have been reading it wrong. We need to turn around and start from the beginning as a people who are desperate for God. If the cross and the internal witness of God's Spirit was enough, then why were the one-hundred twenty disciples compelled to wait for something more? They could have sat around and convinced themselves that there was nothing else worth waiting for. They had salvation, scripture and the Spirit. But as I have heard many times before, it's not about us having Jesus, the Word and the Spirit—it's about Jesus, the Word and the Spirit having us! Unless we're willing to wait as they did in the upper room, we will never come to the place where worship is beckoning us to come.

Holy Spirit come in power
Bringing fire to your sons and daughters
A generation of the cross
Longing for a Pentecost

Fresh fire from heaven let Your flame consume
my life

Let it burn in me
(From the song *A Prayer for Pentecost*
by Jay Walls)

Chapter Twelve

Prepare for the Coming Storm

*The Word of the Lord came to me: 'Son of man,
this is what the Sovereign Lord says . . . the end!
The end has come upon the four corners of the
land. The end is now upon you and I will unleash
my anger against you.'*
Ezekiel 7:2

*And without faith it is impossible to please God,
because anyone who comes to him must believe
that he exists and that he rewards those who
earnestly seek him.*
Hebrews 10:6

I can still remember the day like it was yesterday. April 3, 1974 was an historic day in America. Although I was only seven years old, the memories of that day are still very much etched in my mind. As I had gotten off the school bus, I could see dark clouds in the horizon. My older brother and sister were already home and my parents were still at work. Shortly after I completed my usual afterschool routine the phone rang. On the other end was my mother who demanded we immediately go to the basement. I knew that meant only one thing—a tornado was on its way.

Fortunately, the tornado never reached my neighborhood; but I remember spending much of the night in the basement. That day is forever impressed in my memory as it is for many who lived in Ohio on that spring day. It was the day of the great tornado outbreak, the worst of the storms spawned six F5 tornadoes in our nation's heartland. One town in particular, Xenia, was about fifty miles from where I lived. If you are a student of weather phenomenon, you will have no problem recognizing the name of that city as it became known for enduring one of the most powerful and deadliest tornadoes in history.

Thirty-three people died in Xenia along with thousands injured. A wave of mass destruction was all that was left. Although nothing could have prevented the obliterating damage in the wake of the aftermath, the thirty-three people who lost their lives could possibly have been saved. The most amazing part of Xenia's story rests in one oversight by community officials. Had those officials made a different decision concerning public safety, history may have been changed. Perhaps it was a matter of "it will never happen here" or an issue of "there are more pressing things we need to address," but whatever the reason, the city of Xenia failed to install a warning siren system. I can only imagine how different things may have been for the families of those who had lost loved ones had someone been able to warn them of the coming destructive storm.

As you consider the content of this book, it should be evident that I am attempting to call the church back to a place of legitimate worship in spirit and in truth; however, I must confess that I have an alternative motive in sharing my heart. There is a storm brewing on the horizon and life as we know it, in the comfortable and complacent church of America, is about to experience a wave of unprecedented destruction which will destroy the very foundations we have placed our false sense of trust upon. I am a siren warning of this coming storm and I am crying out to my generation to "PREPARE!" The only thing that will save us from the fury to come is a return to the genuine life of worship before the Lord. For too long we have muddled our way through the Christian faith and compromised all that is sacred and holy for the sake of comfort, convenience and crowds. We have lost the essentials of truth, spirit, humility, sensitivity, prayer, holiness and the fear of the Lord. We've replaced these things with relevancy, entertainment, compromise, strategies and the need to build our own kingdom within the kingdom of God. And for that reason, the Spirit of God is grieved and judgment will begin with the *"house of the Lord"* (1 Peter 4:17).

The prophet Ezekiel cried out to his people that *"The end is now upon you."* As our nation digresses in moral filth and political corruption his statement rings truer than ever. Jesus promised in Matthew 24-25 that there would come a day when the *"end"* would be evident. We are in the beginning of these days—deception, wars, hatred and false prophets. Paul echoes this by adding that these *"last days"* will be filled with people who will be:

> . . . *lovers of themselves, lovers of money, boastful, proud, abusive, disobedient to their parents, ungrateful, unholy, without love, unforgiving, slanderous, without self-control, brutal, not lovers of the good, treacherous, rash, conceited, lovers of pleasure rather than lovers of God—having a form of godliness but denying its power.* (2 Timothy 3:1-6)

Is this not an accurate picture of our world today? Even more, is this not a picture of what we are experiencing in the church?

At this point, you may be asking, "Yes, I know that our world is a mess, but what does the subject of worship have to do with all of this?" As our world increases in wickedness and the end draws near, all of life will center on one primary issue: who will you worship! There will come a day in which we all will have to draw a line in the sand and declare where our loyalties genuinely lie. No longer will we be able to waffle between the sacred and secular in the way we approach our worship of God. No longer will we be able to pretend that Christ is at the center of our lives when we are so dependent upon this world to fulfill our needs, wants and desires.

As the Lord looks upon this world He has created, the one question He poses to us is, *"when the Son of Man comes, will he find faith on the earth?"* (Luke 18:8). The life of faith and the life of worship cannot be separated. One cannot be a person of faith while neglecting to be a worshiper of God. Likewise, one cannot be a genuine worshiper while failing to have faith in the Lord. Hebrews 10:6 states, *"And without faith it is impossible to please God, because anyone who comes to him must believe that he exists and that he rewards those who earnestly seek him."* Without faith, we cannot please God and we cannot have faith unless we believe and seek Him. Faith is more than believing something *about* God; rather, it is a belief *in* God which translates to how we live our lives. True faith reaches the depths of the heart and calls us to act upon what we believe. If I have faith in the Lord, then my life will reflect that He is indeed my Lord.

Prior to writing this book, I began a journey of deepening my faith. On the heels of losing a job and moving to another city in the same weekend, The Lord called me to do the unthinkable. My life prior to this point was miserable. I knew that God has much more for me than what my life was experiencing. I knew that He was beckoning me to go farther with Him than I ever had before, yet I was reluctant to follow. Each day felt like drudgery as I lived in the monotony of purposeless living. Like many, I called myself a worshiper, but the world had too much hold upon me. I looked to it for my needs of provision, joy and pleasure. Now, having a household of seven children and no income, I was left to wallow in a world of self-pity. If asked, I would have testified that I had faith but the reality of what was in my heart testified to another truth—my experience with God was only what I imagined it to be and not what I proclaimed it to be. Although I cannot fully explain it, something happened to me when I heard the words, "You're fired." I had been reading several books about faith, and it was as if God said, "It's time to take your head knowledge and make it heart knowledge." As I walked out the doors of my former employer, I suddenly felt as if God was calling me to walk with Him on a new journey.

As I went to my new home, I sought the Lord. I wanted to know what was next. How would He provide? What did I need to do? How would I take care of my family? As I prayed and waited for

Him to answer, I could only hear one word: nothing. "Nothing?" I thought, "Really God? You have to give me more than this."

After pursuing more of an explanation, God's nothing suddenly became, "I am calling you to live a life of faith." With much anxiety, I surrendered to the Lord's plan and as I did, He directed me to begin a ministry of worship. The more I have pursued this calling, the more I have come to hear the heart of the Father beckoning His people to come back to the place of genuine worship. For over four years, I have journeyed on this walk of faith. I wish I could tell you that it has been easy and that the Lord has come through for every one of my requests for provision, but that hasn't always been the case. Many days I still feel like I have missed God as nothing in my life seems to make sense. In this process, I learned to let go of so many things in life which I thought were necessary in favor of allowing Him to fill those voids. Today, I have a much greater sense of contentment. My journey of faith has begun to bring me to a place where I am no longer living by faith in what God can do for me but living by faith in the God whom I worship.

During those initial days of receiving God's direction for my life, I received a word from the Lord. Deep within my spirit, I heard Him say, "Prepare for the coming storm." Not knowing what would soon transpire within our own country shortly after that, we easily recognized that things were drastically changing in our world. With the beginnings of an economic collapse in America, political upheaval in our country, and the increasing reality that things are only getting worse, the severe storm clouds are on the horizon and are approaching us quickly. More specifically, the Lord made it clear to me that His people need to learn to live by faith in order to endure the fury of this coming storm.

My part in this is to call His people back to genuine worship that produces genuine faith. If we, His people, claim to worship Him and cannot live in a way that reflects our full trust, hope and confidence in Him when life is easy, how will we weather the storm when it bears down upon us? I cannot help to think of Jesus' teaching in Matthew 7:24-27 concerning the two men who chose to build their houses on completely opposite foundations. One man's foundation was destroyed when the storm came while the other man's withstood the calamity of the tempest. As Jesus concluded the Sermon on the Mount with this story, He wanted His disciples to be left with the lingering question of, "What will you choose to build your life upon?"

Rarely is the need to have faith associated with the subject of worship. Our tendency is to categorize the various aspects of our experiences causing us to fail in seeing the connectedness of the Christian life. Worship is not just a piece of the puzzle that is attached to faith; rather, it is like a painted canvas where all the colors of the painting are blended together to create a picture. If the God that I worship cannot be seen as the God He truly is, my portrait will be flawed. It is critical that we return to worship in spirit and in truth as it is the only way to discover the depths of knowing God's heart revealed to us. As long as we fix our eyes upon other things, our faith will never be anything of substance. For too long, the church has made faith an easy acquisition which costs the buyer nothing more than a simple prayer and weekly attendance to Sunday service. Rather than examining the reality of our anemic faith which is evidenced through the lack of the Holy Spirit's presence and power in our midst, we make ourselves feel better by convincing ourselves how much God loves and accepts us despite our shortcomings. I will not dispute our need to know of His love and acceptance, but somewhere along the way, knowing these things should cause us to forsake all that is of this world and passionately pursue His presence with a relentless desire that will stop at nothing to know Him!

This is where worship in spirit and in truth leads—to a place where God is everything and we are nothing. It is a life that is completely "enamored by His presence, humbled by His grace, captured by His endless love, and consumed by His embrace." This is the cry of a heart that is desperate for God and this is the place where faith begins. It's not a matter of *believing* God. It is a life that has come to know the Lord so intimately that you see no reason to seek satisfaction, provision and passion from any other means or any other place. It is the simple expression of saying, "I have all I need in Jesus." Unless we begin to put ourselves in a place where this can become a reality, we will never come to know the depths of the heart of God. Without knowing the heart of the Father, how will we ever find our way through the dark days that lie ahead? If we cannot see God for who He truly is, how will we be able to persevere in trials and tribulations that are certain to arise?

Darkness is beginning to sweep the land. As the intensity of the storm increases, it will become evident as to what foundation we have built our lives upon. The kind of faith that the Son of Man seeks to discover on earth is a faith that sees Him as He is—not what we have attempted to make of Him. Many voices will be calling out during these days deceiving the people of God (Matthew 24). Some of those voices will sound like the Christ we have created in our own image and will satisfy the desires that we have falsely placed our faith upon. Rather than holding on to the Anchor of Our Soul in the midst of the storm, we will reach for the first hand that offers to rescue us from the chaos of life. Faith, however, does not consider circumstance. It is not moved by the notion of self-preservation. It is not confined to the situations of the earthly realm. It looks beyond the reality of the natural and sees an all-powerful, all-knowing, all-present Sovereign God whose ways are higher than our ways. The true worshipers will have clear vision of His face despite being in the darkness. They will hear His voice despite the deafening thunder that surrounds. And when the torrent of the storm is unleashed devastating everything in its path, they will be found holding on to the only thing in life that remains: Jesus Christ!

As I am still learning along this journey of faith, I have found that the most difficult aspect of all of this is letting go of what I want God to be. I want Him to be Provider, Healer and Counselor; yet I fail in my faith when He becomes Discipliner, Master and Judge. God is all of these things and much, much more. If I fail to allow the Lord to be everything that He is to me, I will place my faith in other things. This is our great dilemma! Faith has eyes to see the God who is worthy of all honor, blessing and glory despite anything we may be facing in our lives. By doing so, worship becomes a response in all of life. All that we do, say, think and believe should reflect the truth of God and the Spirit of God living within us.

If we are to become a people of faith, we first need to come to grips with the notion that "nothing good lives in" us—except for Jesus Christ. Why are we so afraid of seeing ourselves for who we truly are? Why are we so afraid to proclaim in our churches that without Christ we are indeed unworthy, miserable and wretched people? I see it much differently. I believe that in knowing that I am nothing without Christ, I am able to appreciate the incomparable worth of my salvation and because of that, I have a greater faith in the only One who brings any value to my life! For faith to arise in our lives, we must also see God for who He truly is. We cannot please God if we do not see Him in any other way. He cannot be reduced to a god of our liking nor can He be made to do our bidding to satisfy our selfish desires. We cannot have faith and ignore His truth—no matter how offensive His truth may be to us. The reality of faith is that either *He is* or *He isn't.* Faith proclaims that if He is God, then He must be God to us in all of life. If He cannot be that for us, then we will become a church whose faith rests upon the opinions, thoughts and ways of man.

Worship comes down to a choice: God or myself. Faith is merely the bridge that connects us to the land where we are choosing to live. Thus, it is impossible for us to have faith in ourselves and faith in God simultaneously. One path leads to the ways, ideas and beliefs of man where we create our own world for God to exist in. In this place, He is worshiped by our standards and contained by our boundaries of comfort and convenience. The other path leads to a place of truth, life and freedom. In this place, the King reigns supreme and all that He has made known about Himself is revered, honored and worshiped. Here, God has no boundaries and His power, majesty and glory permeates all of life. Those who fix their eyes upon their King no longer desire to look anywhere else as they are captivated by the gaze of His heart. In that moment when their eyes meet, the impossible becomes possible as God becomes everything and nothing else in all of life matters.

The time has come to let go of all that has held us back from truly beholding the heart of the Father. We will become like the man who built his house on shifting sands only to be washed away in the coming storm. Whether we like it or not, our faith will be tested and tried beyond what we have ever experienced. The storm is coming and terrible times will follow. When that day comes, the spirit and truth of our worship will be made known. All that God is and who we have let Him be to our lives will become evident. When all is said and done, what will be said of our lives in regards to how we worshiped the Lord? Which land will our bridge of faith take us to live in?

The genuine call to worship is one that says, "*He must become greater and I must become less*" (John 3:30). It is the forsaking of one's life for the sake of living a life for Jesus Christ. We've made it too much about ourselves, we've stolen center stage and we have forgotten our First love to love lesser things. I can only be a voice which calls forth a hungry people who would desire to forsake the things of this world to enter into another world—one of Spirit and of truth. This world can no longer hold my affections nor demand my attention. Time is too short.

My prayer is for your heart to cry out for true worship to be restored to the people of God. Let those who worship the Lord do so in worshiping Him in spirit and in truth. In examining everything that has gone wrong with worship, I pray that we would once again discover what needs to be made right in worship: to once again become a people who are wholly captivated in all of life with our Lord Jesus Christ. I leave you with these final thoughts from my song *Heart's Cry* and may they become the cry of your heart as well:

You are holy, awesome in power
And I long to know you Lord
My insatiable desire
You are worthy, faithful and true
Let the cry of my heart
Burn with passion for you

Enamored by your presence
Humbled by Your grace
Captured by Your endless love
Consumed by Your embrace

You are Jesus, Savior and King
I abandon myself to You
I give You everything
You are worthy, faithful and true
Let the cry of my heart
Burn with passion for you

(To hear this song visit:
www.jtwalls.blogspot.com)

Endnotes

1   A.W. Tozer, *Whatever Happened to Worship?* (Camp Hill: Christian Publications, 1985), 38.

2   Ibid., 44.

3   Andrew E. Hill, *Enter His Courts With Praise* (Grand Rapids: Baker Books, 1993), 25.

4   John MacArthur, *Fools Gold?* (Wheaton: Crossway Books, 2005), 38.

5   D.A. Carson, *The Difficult Doctrine of the Love of God* (Wheaton: Crossway Books, 2000), 41.

6   David F. Wells, *God in the Wasteland* (Grand Rapids: Eerdmans, 1994), 90.

7   A.W. Tozer, *The Knowledge of the Holy* (San Francisco: Harper and Row, 1961), 69.

8   Bob Kauflin, *Worship Matters* (Wheaton: Crossway Books, 2008), 161.

9   Ibid., 160-161.

10   David F. Wells, *God in the Wasteland* (Grand Rapids: Eerdmans, 1994), 116.

11   A. W. Tozer, *The Pursuit of God* (Camp Hill: Christian Publications, 1982), 101.

12   Edward F. Murphy, *The Handbook for Spiritual Warfare* (Nashville: Thomas Nelson, 1992), 24.

13   A. W. Tozer, *The Warfare of the Spirit* (Camp Hill: Christian Publications, 1993), 3.

14   John Bevere, *The Fear of the Lord* (Lake Mary: Charisma House, 2006), 78.

15   A.W. Tozer, *Whatever Happened to Worship?* (Camp Hill: Christian Publications, 1985), 76.

16   Ibid., 76.

17   Nancy Leigh DeMoss, *Holiness* (Chicago: Moody Press, 2005), 22.

18 A.W. Tozer, *The Pursuit of Man* (Camp Hill: Christian Publications, 1978), 112.

19 Blue Letter Bible.

20 Andrew Murray, *With Christ in the School of Prayer* (New Kensington: Whitaker House, 1981), 25.

21 E.M. Bounds, *The Complete Works of E.M. Bounds on Prayer* (Grand Rapids: Baker Books, 1990), 30.

22 Ibid., 31.

23 Alfred Edersheim, *The Life and Times of Jesus the Messiah* (Peabody: Hendrickson, 1993), 501.

24 John N. Oswalt, *The NIV Application Commentary: Isaiah* (Grand Rapids: Zondervan, 2003), 624.

25 Joseph Blenkinsopp, *The Anchor Bible: Isaiah 56-66* (New York: Doubleday, 2003), 182-183.

26 J. Alec Motyer, *The Prophecy of Isaiah* (Downers Grove: InterVarsity Press, 1993), 478.

27 William Sanford LaSor, *Old Testament Survey* (Grand Rapids: Eerdmans, 1996), 308-309.

28 Abraham J. Heschel, *The Prophets* (New York: Harper and Row, 1962), 198.

29 John N. Oswalt, *The NIV Application Commentary: Isaiah*, 625.

30 J. Alec Motyer, *The Prophecy of Isaiah* (Downers Grove: InterVarsity Press, 1993), 480.

31 Dallas Willard, *The Spirit of the Disciplines* (New York: HarperOne, 1988), 134.

32 Francis Chan, *Forgotten God* (Colorado Springs: David C. Cook, 2009), 15.

About the Author

For over twenty-five years, Jay Walls has served as a worship leader calling the church to a more intimate experience with Christ. In 2007, the Lord called Jay to step out in faith and begin True Life Worship Ministries. This ministry seeks to bring restoration, healing and freedom to the Body of Christ through prophetic worship and teaching that focuses on the need for the people of God to return to seeking the Father in spirit and in truth. Jay's blog (found below) provides a biblical and theological look at the subject of worship in light of the prevailing practices, philosophies and worldviews that are affecting the body of Christ. Jay holds a B.A. in Bible and Theology from Central Bible College, a MAR in Worship Studies and an MDIV in Professional Ministries from Liberty University in Lynchburg, Virginia.

As a singer and songwriter, Jay's songs reveal God's love, grace, mercy and power aimed to liberate and transform lives drawing people to the heart of God. Jay grew up in Columbus, Ohio and now resides in Belgium, Wisconsin with his wife and seven children. He currently serves as a worship leader and elder at New Season Community Church. In his spare time, Jay enjoys gourmet cooking, traveling, football and mostly, spending time with his family.

True Life Worship Ministries

www.jtwalls.blogspot.com
truelifeworshipministries@live.com